C-4808   CAREER EXAMINATION SERIES

This is your
PASSBOOK for...

Wastewater Treatment Mechanic

Test Preparation Study Guide
Questions & Answers

COPYRIGHT NOTICE

This book is SOLELY intended for, is sold ONLY to, and its use is RESTRICTED to individual, bona fide applicants or candidates who qualify by virtue of having seriously filed applications for appropriate license, certificate, professional and/or promotional advancement, higher school matriculation, scholarship, or other legitimate requirements of education and/or governmental authorities.

This book is NOT intended for use, class instruction, tutoring, training, duplication, copying, reprinting, excerption, or adaptation, etc., by:

1) Other publishers
2) Proprietors and/or Instructors of "Coaching" and/or Preparatory Courses
3) Personnel and/or Training Divisions of commercial, industrial, and governmental organizations
4) Schools, colleges, or universities and/or their departments and staffs, including teachers and other personnel
5) Testing Agencies or Bureaus
6) Study groups which seek by the purchase of a single volume to copy and/or duplicate and/or adapt this material for use by the group as a whole without having purchased individual volumes for each of the members of the group
7) Et al.

Such persons would be in violation of appropriate Federal and State statutes.

PROVISION OF LICENSING AGREEMENTS – Recognized educational, commercial, industrial, and governmental institutions and organizations, and others legitimately engaged in educational pursuits, including training, testing, and measurement activities, may address request for a licensing agreement to the copyright owners, who will determine whether, and under what conditions, including fees and charges, the materials in this book may be used them. In other words, a licensing facility exists for the legitimate use of the material in this book on other than an individual basis. However, it is asseverated and affirmed here that the material in this book CANNOT be used without the receipt of the express permission of such a licensing agreement from the Publishers. Inquiries re licensing should be addressed to the company, attention rights and permissions department.

All rights reserved, including the right of reproduction in whole or in part, in any form or by any means, electronic or mechanical, including photocopying, recording, or by any information storage and retrieval system, without permission in writing from the Publisher.

Copyright © 2025 by
National Learning Corporation

212 Michael Drive, Syosset, NY 11791
(516) 921-8888 • www.passbooks.com
E-mail: info@passbooks.com

PASSBOOK® SERIES

THE *PASSBOOK® SERIES* has been created to prepare applicants and candidates for the ultimate academic battlefield – the examination room.

At some time in our lives, each and every one of us may be required to take an examination – for validation, matriculation, admission, qualification, registration, certification, or licensure.

Based on the assumption that every applicant or candidate has met the basic formal educational standards, has taken the required number of courses, and read the necessary texts, the *PASSBOOK® SERIES* furnishes the one special preparation which may assure passing with confidence, instead of failing with insecurity. Examination questions – together with answers – are furnished as the basic vehicle for study so that the mysteries of the examination and its compounding difficulties may be eliminated or diminished by a sure method.

This book is meant to help you pass your examination provided that you qualify and are serious in your objective.

The entire field is reviewed through the huge store of content information which is succinctly presented through a provocative and challenging approach – the question-and-answer method.

A climate of success is established by furnishing the correct answers at the end of each test.

You soon learn to recognize types of questions, forms of questions, and patterns of questioning. You may even begin to anticipate expected outcomes.

You perceive that many questions are repeated or adapted so that you can gain acute insights, which may enable you to score many sure points.

You learn how to confront new questions, or types of questions, and to attack them confidently and work out the correct answers.

You note objectives and emphases, and recognize pitfalls and dangers, so that you may make positive educational adjustments.

Moreover, you are kept fully informed in relation to new concepts, methods, practices, and directions in the field.

You discover that you are actually taking the examination all the time: you are preparing for the examination by "taking" an examination, not by reading extraneous and/or supererogatory textbooks.

In short, this PASSBOOK®, used directedly, should be an important factor in helping you to pass your test.

WASTEWATER TREATMENT MECHANIC

DUTIES:
A Wastewater Treatment Mechanic performs a variety of skilled tasks in maintaining, overhauling and assembling mechanical equipment and auxiliaries associated with combustion equipment, boilers, cryogenic equipment, large diesel engines, pumps, compressors, barscreens, collectors, clarifiers, centrifuges, conveyors, heat exchangers, emissions control equipment, and other equipment found in a wastewater treatment plant or a wastewater collection system; or performs the more difficult and skilled mechanical work with limited supervisory responsibility over a small crew.

SCOPE OF THE EXAMINATION
The examination will consist entirely of a multiple-choice written test in which candidates may be examined for knowledge of: principles, operation, maintenance, repair, adjustment, and service of blowers, fans, pumps, and auxiliaries; methods of repair and overhaul of centrifuges, blowers, gas and air-compressor units, pumps, gear drivers, and boilers; methods, equipment, tools, and terminology of trades involved in mechanical repair work; safety principles and practices related to maintenance and repair of wastewater equipment; the ability to: read and follow blueprints, plans, and written instructions; troubleshoot mechanical problems and equipment; deal tactfully and effectively with others; and other necessary skills, knowledge, and abilities.

HOW TO TAKE A TEST

I. YOU MUST PASS AN EXAMINATION

A. *WHAT EVERY CANDIDATE SHOULD KNOW*

Examination applicants often ask us for help in preparing for the written test. What can I study in advance? What kinds of questions will be asked? How will the test be given? How will the papers be graded?

As an applicant for a civil service examination, you may be wondering about some of these things. Our purpose here is to suggest effective methods of advance study and to describe civil service examinations.

Your chances for success on this examination can be increased if you know how to prepare. Those "pre-examination jitters" can be reduced if you know what to expect. You can even experience an adventure in good citizenship if you know why civil service exams are given.

B. *WHY ARE CIVIL SERVICE EXAMINATIONS GIVEN?*

Civil service examinations are important to you in two ways. As a citizen, you want public jobs filled by employees who know how to do their work. As a job seeker, you want a fair chance to compete for that job on an equal footing with other candidates. The best-known means of accomplishing this two-fold goal is the competitive examination.

Exams are widely publicized throughout the nation. They may be administered for jobs in federal, state, city, municipal, town or village governments or agencies.

Any citizen may apply, with some limitations, such as the age or residence of applicants. Your experience and education may be reviewed to see whether you meet the requirements for the particular examination. When these requirements exist, they are reasonable and applied consistently to all applicants. Thus, a competitive examination may cause you some uneasiness now, but it is your privilege and safeguard.

C. *HOW ARE CIVIL SERVICE EXAMS DEVELOPED?*

Examinations are carefully written by trained technicians who are specialists in the field known as "psychological measurement," in consultation with recognized authorities in the field of work that the test will cover. These experts recommend the subject matter areas or skills to be tested; only those knowledges or skills important to your success on the job are included. The most reliable books and source materials available are used as references. Together, the experts and technicians judge the difficulty level of the questions.

Test technicians know how to phrase questions so that the problem is clearly stated. Their ethics do not permit "trick" or "catch" questions. Questions may have been tried out on sample groups, or subjected to statistical analysis, to determine their usefulness.

Written tests are often used in combination with performance tests, ratings of training and experience, and oral interviews. All of these measures combine to form the best-known means of finding the right person for the right job.

II. HOW TO PASS THE WRITTEN TEST

A. NATURE OF THE EXAMINATION

To prepare intelligently for civil service examinations, you should know how they differ from school examinations you have taken. In school you were assigned certain definite pages to read or subjects to cover. The examination questions were quite detailed and usually emphasized memory. Civil service exams, on the other hand, try to discover your present ability to perform the duties of a position, plus your potentiality to learn these duties. In other words, a civil service exam attempts to predict how successful you will be. Questions cover such a broad area that they cannot be as minute and detailed as school exam questions.

In the public service similar kinds of work, or positions, are grouped together in one "class." This process is known as *position-classification*. All the positions in a class are paid according to the salary range for that class. One class title covers all of these positions, and they are all tested by the same examination.

B. FOUR BASIC STEPS

1) Study the announcement

How, then, can you know what subjects to study? Our best answer is: "Learn as much as possible about the class of positions for which you've applied." The exam will test the knowledge, skills and abilities needed to do the work.

Your most valuable source of information about the position you want is the official exam announcement. This announcement lists the training and experience qualifications. Check these standards and apply only if you come reasonably close to meeting them.

The brief description of the position in the examination announcement offers some clues to the subjects which will be tested. Think about the job itself. Review the duties in your mind. Can you perform them, or are there some in which you are rusty? Fill in the blank spots in your preparation.

Many jurisdictions preview the written test in the exam announcement by including a section called "Knowledge and Abilities Required," "Scope of the Examination," or some similar heading. Here you will find out specifically what fields will be tested.

2) Review your own background

Once you learn in general what the position is all about, and what you need to know to do the work, ask yourself which subjects you already know fairly well and which need improvement. You may wonder whether to concentrate on improving your strong areas or on building some background in your fields of weakness. When the announcement has specified "some knowledge" or "considerable knowledge," or has used adjectives like "beginning principles of…" or "advanced … methods," you can get a clue as to the number and difficulty of questions to be asked in any given field. More questions, and hence broader coverage, would be included for those subjects which are more important in the work. Now weigh your strengths and weaknesses against the job requirements and prepare accordingly.

3) Determine the level of the position

Another way to tell how intensively you should prepare is to understand the level of the job for which you are applying. Is it the entering level? In other words, is this the position in which beginners in a field of work are hired? Or is it an intermediate or advanced level? Sometimes this is indicated by such words as "Junior" or "Senior" in the class title. Other jurisdictions use Roman numerals to designate the level – Clerk I, Clerk II, for example. The word "Supervisor" sometimes appears in the title. If the level is not indicated by the title, check the description of duties. Will you be working under very close supervision, or will you have responsibility for independent decisions in this work?

4) Choose appropriate study materials

Now that you know the subjects to be examined and the relative amount of each subject to be covered, you can choose suitable study materials. For beginning level jobs, or even advanced ones, if you have a pronounced weakness in some aspect of your training, read a modern, standard textbook in that field. Be sure it is up to date and has general coverage. Such books are normally available at your library, and the librarian will be glad to help you locate one. For entry-level positions, questions of appropriate difficulty are chosen – neither highly advanced questions, nor those too simple. Such questions require careful thought but not advanced training.

If the position for which you are applying is technical or advanced, you will read more advanced, specialized material. If you are already familiar with the basic principles of your field, elementary textbooks would waste your time. Concentrate on advanced textbooks and technical periodicals. Think through the concepts and review difficult problems in your field.

These are all general sources. You can get more ideas on your own initiative, following these leads. For example, training manuals and publications of the government agency which employs workers in your field can be useful, particularly for technical and professional positions. A letter or visit to the government department involved may result in more specific study suggestions, and certainly will provide you with a more definite idea of the exact nature of the position you are seeking.

III. KINDS OF TESTS

Tests are used for purposes other than measuring knowledge and ability to perform specified duties. For some positions, it is equally important to test ability to make adjustments to new situations or to profit from training. In others, basic mental abilities not dependent on information are essential. Questions which test these things may not appear as pertinent to the duties of the position as those which test for knowledge and information. Yet they are often highly important parts of a fair examination. For very general questions, it is almost impossible to help you direct your study efforts. What we can do is to point out some of the more common of these general abilities needed in public service positions and describe some typical questions.

1) General information

Broad, general information has been found useful for predicting job success in some kinds of work. This is tested in a variety of ways, from vocabulary lists to questions about current events. Basic background in some field of work, such as sociology or economics, may be sampled in a group of questions. Often these are principles which have become familiar to most persons through exposure rather than through formal training. It is difficult to advise you how to study for these questions; being alert to the world around you is our best suggestion.

2) Verbal ability

An example of an ability needed in many positions is verbal or language ability. Verbal ability is, in brief, the ability to use and understand words. Vocabulary and grammar tests are typical measures of this ability. Reading comprehension or paragraph interpretation questions are common in many kinds of civil service tests. You are given a paragraph of written material and asked to find its central meaning.

3) Numerical ability

Number skills can be tested by the familiar arithmetic problem, by checking paired lists of numbers to see which are alike and which are different, or by interpreting charts and graphs. In the latter test, a graph may be printed in the test booklet which you are asked to use as the basis for answering questions.

4) Observation

A popular test for law-enforcement positions is the observation test. A picture is shown to you for several minutes, then taken away. Questions about the picture test your ability to observe both details and larger elements.

5) Following directions

In many positions in the public service, the employee must be able to carry out written instructions dependably and accurately. You may be given a chart with several columns, each column listing a variety of information. The questions require you to carry out directions involving the information given in the chart.

6) Skills and aptitudes

Performance tests effectively measure some manual skills and aptitudes. When the skill is one in which you are trained, such as typing or shorthand, you can practice. These tests are often very much like those given in business school or high school courses. For many of the other skills and aptitudes, however, no short-time preparation can be made. Skills and abilities natural to you or that you have developed throughout your lifetime are being tested.

Many of the general questions just described provide all the data needed to answer the questions and ask you to use your reasoning ability to find the answers. Your best preparation for these tests, as well as for tests of facts and ideas, is to be at your physical and mental best. You, no doubt, have your own methods of getting into an exam-taking mood and keeping "in shape." The next section lists some ideas on this subject.

IV. KINDS OF QUESTIONS

Only rarely is the "essay" question, which you answer in narrative form, used in civil service tests. Civil service tests are usually of the short-answer type. Full instructions for answering these questions will be given to you at the examination. But in case this is your first experience with short-answer questions and separate answer sheets, here is what you need to know:

1) **Multiple-choice Questions**

Most popular of the short-answer questions is the "multiple choice" or "best answer" question. It can be used, for example, to test for factual knowledge, ability to solve problems or judgment in meeting situations found at work.

A multiple-choice question is normally one of three types—
- It can begin with an incomplete statement followed by several possible endings. You are to find the one ending which *best* completes the statement, although some of the others may not be entirely wrong.
- It can also be a complete statement in the form of a question which is answered by choosing one of the statements listed.

- It can be in the form of a problem – again you select the best answer.

Here is an example of a multiple-choice question with a discussion which should give you some clues as to the method for choosing the right answer:

When an employee has a complaint about his assignment, the action which will *best* help him overcome his difficulty is to
- A. discuss his difficulty with his coworkers
- B. take the problem to the head of the organization
- C. take the problem to the person who gave him the assignment
- D. say nothing to anyone about his complaint

In answering this question, you should study each of the choices to find which is best. Consider choice "A" – Certainly an employee may discuss his complaint with fellow employees, but no change or improvement can result, and the complaint remains unresolved. Choice "B" is a poor choice since the head of the organization probably does not know what assignment you have been given, and taking your problem to him is known as "going over the head" of the supervisor. The supervisor, or person who made the assignment, is the person who can clarify it or correct any injustice. Choice "C" is, therefore, correct. To say nothing, as in choice "D," is unwise. Supervisors have and interest in knowing the problems employees are facing, and the employee is seeking a solution to his problem.

2) True/False Questions

The "true/false" or "right/wrong" form of question is sometimes used. Here a complete statement is given. Your job is to decide whether the statement is right or wrong.

SAMPLE: A roaming cell-phone call to a nearby city costs less than a non-roaming call to a distant city.

This statement is wrong, or false, since roaming calls are more expensive.

This is not a complete list of all possible question forms, although most of the others are variations of these common types. You will always get complete directions for answering questions. Be sure you understand *how* to mark your answers – ask questions until you do.

V. RECORDING YOUR ANSWERS

Computer terminals are used more and more today for many different kinds of exams.
For an examination with very few applicants, you may be told to record your answers in the test booklet itself. Separate answer sheets are much more common. If this separate answer sheet is to be scored by machine – and this is often the case – it is highly important that you mark your answers correctly in order to get credit.
An electronic scoring machine is often used in civil service offices because of the speed with which papers can be scored. Machine-scored answer sheets must be marked with a pencil, which will be given to you. This pencil has a high graphite content which responds to the electronic scoring machine. As a matter of fact, stray dots may register as answers, so do not let your pencil rest on the answer sheet while you are pondering the correct answer. Also, if your pencil lead breaks or is otherwise defective, ask for another.

Since the answer sheet will be dropped in a slot in the scoring machine, be careful not to bend the corners or get the paper crumpled.

The answer sheet normally has five vertical columns of numbers, with 30 numbers to a column. These numbers correspond to the question numbers in your test booklet. After each number, going across the page are four or five pairs of dotted lines. These short dotted lines have small letters or numbers above them. The first two pairs may also have a "T" or "F" above the letters. This indicates that the first two pairs only are to be used if the questions are of the true-false type. If the questions are multiple choice, disregard the "T" and "F" and pay attention only to the small letters or numbers.

Answer your questions in the manner of the sample that follows:

32. The largest city in the United States is
    A. Washington, D.C.
    B. New York City
    C. Chicago
    D. Detroit
    E. San Francisco

1) Choose the answer you think is best. (New York City is the largest, so "B" is correct.)
2) Find the row of dotted lines numbered the same as the question you are answering. (Find row number 32)
3) Find the pair of dotted lines corresponding to the answer. (Find the pair of lines under the mark "B.")
4) Make a solid black mark between the dotted lines.

VI. BEFORE THE TEST

Common sense will help you find procedures to follow to get ready for an examination. Too many of us, however, overlook these sensible measures. Indeed, nervousness and fatigue have been found to be the most serious reasons why applicants fail to do their best on civil service tests. Here is a list of reminders:

- Begin your preparation early – Don't wait until the last minute to go scurrying around for books and materials or to find out what the position is all about.
- Prepare continuously – An hour a night for a week is better than an all-night cram session. This has been definitely established. What is more, a night a week for a month will return better dividends than crowding your study into a shorter period of time.
- Locate the place of the exam – You have been sent a notice telling you when and where to report for the examination. If the location is in a different town or otherwise unfamiliar to you, it would be well to inquire the best route and learn something about the building.
- Relax the night before the test – Allow your mind to rest. Do not study at all that night. Plan some mild recreation or diversion; then go to bed early and get a good night's sleep.
- Get up early enough to make a leisurely trip to the place for the test – This way unforeseen events, traffic snarls, unfamiliar buildings, etc. will not upset you.
- Dress comfortably – A written test is not a fashion show. You will be known by number and not by name, so wear something comfortable.

- Leave excess paraphernalia at home – Shopping bags and odd bundles will get in your way. You need bring only the items mentioned in the official notice you received; usually everything you need is provided. Do not bring reference books to the exam. They will only confuse those last minutes and be taken away from you when in the test room.
- Arrive somewhat ahead of time – If because of transportation schedules you must get there very early, bring a newspaper or magazine to take your mind off yourself while waiting.
- Locate the examination room – When you have found the proper room, you will be directed to the seat or part of the room where you will sit. Sometimes you are given a sheet of instructions to read while you are waiting. Do not fill out any forms until you are told to do so; just read them and be prepared.
- Relax and prepare to listen to the instructions
- If you have any physical problem that may keep you from doing your best, be sure to tell the test administrator. If you are sick or in poor health, you really cannot do your best on the exam. You can come back and take the test some other time.

VII. AT THE TEST

The day of the test is here and you have the test booklet in your hand. The temptation to get going is very strong. Caution! There is more to success than knowing the right answers. You must know how to identify your papers and understand variations in the type of short-answer question used in this particular examination. Follow these suggestions for maximum results from your efforts:

1) Cooperate with the monitor
The test administrator has a duty to create a situation in which you can be as much at ease as possible. He will give instructions, tell you when to begin, check to see that you are marking your answer sheet correctly, and so on. He is not there to guard you, although he will see that your competitors do not take unfair advantage. He wants to help you do your best.

2) Listen to all instructions
Don't jump the gun! Wait until you understand all directions. In most civil service tests you get more time than you need to answer the questions. So don't be in a hurry. Read each word of instructions until you clearly understand the meaning. Study the examples, listen to all announcements and follow directions. Ask questions if you do not understand what to do.

3) Identify your papers
Civil service exams are usually identified by number only. You will be assigned a number; you must not put your name on your test papers. Be sure to copy your number correctly. Since more than one exam may be given, copy your exact examination title.

4) Plan your time
Unless you are told that a test is a "speed" or "rate of work" test, speed itself is usually not important. Time enough to answer all the questions will be provided, but this does not mean that you have all day. An overall time limit has been set. Divide the total time (in minutes) by the number of questions to determine the approximate time you have for each question.

5) Do not linger over difficult questions

If you come across a difficult question, mark it with a paper clip (useful to have along) and come back to it when you have been through the booklet. One caution if you do this – be sure to skip a number on your answer sheet as well. Check often to be sure that you have not lost your place and that you are marking in the row numbered the same as the question you are answering.

6) Read the questions

Be sure you know what the question asks! Many capable people are unsuccessful because they failed to *read* the questions correctly.

7) Answer all questions

Unless you have been instructed that a penalty will be deducted for incorrect answers, it is better to guess than to omit a question.

8) Speed tests

It is often better NOT to guess on speed tests. It has been found that on timed tests people are tempted to spend the last few seconds before time is called in marking answers at random – without even reading them – in the hope of picking up a few extra points. To discourage this practice, the instructions may warn you that your score will be "corrected" for guessing. That is, a penalty will be applied. The incorrect answers will be deducted from the correct ones, or some other penalty formula will be used.

9) Review your answers

If you finish before time is called, go back to the questions you guessed or omitted to give them further thought. Review other answers if you have time.

10) Return your test materials

If you are ready to leave before others have finished or time is called, take ALL your materials to the monitor and leave quietly. Never take any test material with you. The monitor can discover whose papers are not complete, and taking a test booklet may be grounds for disqualification.

VIII. EXAMINATION TECHNIQUES

1) Read the general instructions carefully. These are usually printed on the first page of the exam booklet. As a rule, these instructions refer to the timing of the examination; the fact that you should not start work until the signal and must stop work at a signal, etc. If there are any *special* instructions, such as a choice of questions to be answered, make sure that you note this instruction carefully.

2) When you are ready to start work on the examination, that is as soon as the signal has been given, read the instructions to each question booklet, underline any key words or phrases, such as *least, best, outline, describe* and the like. In this way you will tend to answer as requested rather than discover on reviewing your paper that you *listed without describing*, that you selected the *worst* choice rather than the *best* choice, etc.

3) If the examination is of the objective or multiple-choice type – that is, each question will also give a series of possible answers: A, B, C or D, and you are called upon to select the best answer and write the letter next to that answer on your answer paper – it is advisable to start answering each question in turn. There may be anywhere from 50 to 100 such questions in the three or four hours allotted and you can see how much time would be taken if you read through all the questions before beginning to answer any. Furthermore, if you come across a question or group of questions which you know would be difficult to answer, it would undoubtedly affect your handling of all the other questions.

4) If the examination is of the essay type and contains but a few questions, it is a moot point as to whether you should read all the questions before starting to answer any one. Of course, if you are given a choice – say five out of seven and the like – then it is essential to read all the questions so you can eliminate the two that are most difficult. If, however, you are asked to answer all the questions, there may be danger in trying to answer the easiest one first because you may find that you will spend too much time on it. The best technique is to answer the first question, then proceed to the second, etc.

5) Time your answers. Before the exam begins, write down the time it started, then add the time allowed for the examination and write down the time it must be completed, then divide the time available somewhat as follows:
    - If 3-1/2 hours are allowed, that would be 210 minutes. If you have 80 objective-type questions, that would be an average of 2-1/2 minutes per question. Allow yourself no more than 2 minutes per question, or a total of 160 minutes, which will permit about 50 minutes to review.
    - If for the time allotment of 210 minutes there are 7 essay questions to answer, that would average about 30 minutes a question. Give yourself only 25 minutes per question so that you have about 35 minutes to review.

6) The most important instruction is to *read each question* and make sure you know what is wanted. The second most important instruction is to *time yourself properly* so that you answer every question. The third most important instruction is to *answer every question*. Guess if you have to but include something for each question. Remember that you will receive no credit for a blank and will probably receive some credit if you write something in answer to an essay question. If you guess a letter – say "B" for a multiple-choice question – you may have guessed right. If you leave a blank as an answer to a multiple-choice question, the examiners may respect your feelings but it will not add a point to your score. Some exams may penalize you for wrong answers, so in such cases *only*, you may not want to guess unless you have some basis for your answer.

7) Suggestions
    a. Objective-type questions
        1. Examine the question booklet for proper sequence of pages and questions
        2. Read all instructions carefully
        3. Skip any question which seems too difficult; return to it after all other questions have been answered
        4. Apportion your time properly; do not spend too much time on any single question or group of questions

5. Note and underline key words – *all, most, fewest, least, best, worst, same, opposite*, etc.
6. Pay particular attention to negatives
7. Note unusual option, e.g., unduly long, short, complex, different or similar in content to the body of the question
8. Observe the use of "hedging" words – *probably, may, most likely*, etc.
9. Make sure that your answer is put next to the same number as the question
10. Do not second-guess unless you have good reason to believe the second answer is definitely more correct
11. Cross out original answer if you decide another answer is more accurate; do not erase until you are ready to hand your paper in
12. Answer all questions; guess unless instructed otherwise
13. Leave time for review

b. Essay questions
1. Read each question carefully
2. Determine exactly what is wanted. Underline key words or phrases.
3. Decide on outline or paragraph answer
4. Include many different points and elements unless asked to develop any one or two points or elements
5. Show impartiality by giving pros and cons unless directed to select one side only
6. Make and write down any assumptions you find necessary to answer the questions
7. Watch your English, grammar, punctuation and choice of words
8. Time your answers; don't crowd material

8) Answering the essay question

Most essay questions can be answered by framing the specific response around several key words or ideas. Here are a few such key words or ideas:

M's: manpower, materials, methods, money, management
P's: purpose, program, policy, plan, procedure, practice, problems, pitfalls, personnel, public relations
  a. Six basic steps in handling problems:
   1. Preliminary plan and background development
   2. Collect information, data and facts
   3. Analyze and interpret information, data and facts
   4. Analyze and develop solutions as well as make recommendations
   5. Prepare report and sell recommendations
   6. Install recommendations and follow up effectiveness

  b. Pitfalls to avoid
   1. *Taking things for granted* – A statement of the situation does not necessarily imply that each of the elements is necessarily true; for example, a complaint may be invalid and biased so that all that can be taken for granted is that a complaint has been registered

2. *Considering only one side of a situation* – Wherever possible, indicate several alternatives and then point out the reasons you selected the best one
3. *Failing to indicate follow up* – Whenever your answer indicates action on your part, make certain that you will take proper follow-up action to see how successful your recommendations, procedures or actions turn out to be
4. *Taking too long in answering any single question* – Remember to time your answers properly

IX. AFTER THE TEST

Scoring procedures differ in detail among civil service jurisdictions although the general principles are the same. Whether the papers are hand-scored or graded by machine we have described, they are nearly always graded by number. That is, the person who marks the paper knows only the number – never the name – of the applicant. Not until all the papers have been graded will they be matched with names. If other tests, such as training and experience or oral interview ratings have been given, scores will be combined. Different parts of the examination usually have different weights. For example, the written test might count 60 percent of the final grade, and a rating of training and experience 40 percent. In many jurisdictions, veterans will have a certain number of points added to their grades.

After the final grade has been determined, the names are placed in grade order and an eligible list is established. There are various methods for resolving ties between those who get the same final grade – probably the most common is to place first the name of the person whose application was received first. Job offers are made from the eligible list in the order the names appear on it. You will be notified of your grade and your rank as soon as all these computations have been made. This will be done as rapidly as possible.

People who are found to meet the requirements in the announcement are called "eligibles." Their names are put on a list of eligible candidates. An eligible's chances of getting a job depend on how high he stands on this list and how fast agencies are filling jobs from the list.

When a job is to be filled from a list of eligibles, the agency asks for the names of people on the list of eligibles for that job. When the civil service commission receives this request, it sends to the agency the names of the three people highest on this list. Or, if the job to be filled has specialized requirements, the office sends the agency the names of the top three persons who meet these requirements from the general list.

The appointing officer makes a choice from among the three people whose names were sent to him. If the selected person accepts the appointment, the names of the others are put back on the list to be considered for future openings.

That is the rule in hiring from all kinds of eligible lists, whether they are for typist, carpenter, chemist, or something else. For every vacancy, the appointing officer has his choice of any one of the top three eligibles on the list. This explains why the person whose name is on top of the list sometimes does not get an appointment when some of the persons lower on the list do. If the appointing officer chooses the second or third eligible, the No. 1 eligible does not get a job at once, but stays on the list until he is appointed or the list is terminated.

X. HOW TO PASS THE INTERVIEW TEST

The examination for which you applied requires an oral interview test. You have already taken the written test and you are now being called for the interview test – the final part of the formal examination.

You may think that it is not possible to prepare for an interview test and that there are no procedures to follow during an interview. Our purpose is to point out some things you can do in advance that will help you and some good rules to follow and pitfalls to avoid while you are being interviewed.

What is an interview supposed to test?

The written examination is designed to test the technical knowledge and competence of the candidate; the oral is designed to evaluate intangible qualities, not readily measured otherwise, and to establish a list showing the relative fitness of each candidate – as measured against his competitors – for the position sought. Scoring is not on the basis of "right" and "wrong," but on a sliding scale of values ranging from "not passable" to "outstanding." As a matter of fact, it is possible to achieve a relatively low score without a single "incorrect" answer because of evident weakness in the qualities being measured.

Occasionally, an examination may consist entirely of an oral test – either an individual or a group oral. In such cases, information is sought concerning the technical knowledges and abilities of the candidate, since there has been no written examination for this purpose. More commonly, however, an oral test is used to supplement a written examination.

Who conducts interviews?

The composition of oral boards varies among different jurisdictions. In nearly all, a representative of the personnel department serves as chairman. One of the members of the board may be a representative of the department in which the candidate would work. In some cases, "outside experts" are used, and, frequently, a businessman or some other representative of the general public is asked to serve. Labor and management or other special groups may be represented. The aim is to secure the services of experts in the appropriate field.

However the board is composed, it is a good idea (and not at all improper or unethical) to ascertain in advance of the interview who the members are and what groups they represent. When you are introduced to them, you will have some idea of their backgrounds and interests, and at least you will not stutter and stammer over their names.

What should be done before the interview?

While knowledge about the board members is useful and takes some of the surprise element out of the interview, there is other preparation which is more substantive. It *is* possible to prepare for an oral interview – in several ways:

1) Keep a copy of your application and review it carefully before the interview

This may be the only document before the oral board, and the starting point of the interview. Know what education and experience you have listed there, and the sequence and dates of all of it. Sometimes the board will ask you to review the highlights of your experience for them; you should not have to hem and haw doing it.

2) Study the class specification and the examination announcement

Usually, the oral board has one or both of these to guide them. The qualities, characteristics or knowledges required by the position sought are stated in these documents. They offer valuable clues as to the nature of the oral interview. For example, if the job involves supervisory responsibilities, the announcement will usually indicate that knowledge of modern supervisory methods and the qualifications of the candidate as a supervisor will be tested. If so, you can expect such questions, frequently in the form of a hypothetical situation which you are expected to solve. NEVER go into an oral without knowledge of the duties and responsibilities of the job you seek.

3) Think through each qualification required

Try to visualize the kind of questions you would ask if you were a board member. How well could you answer them? Try especially to appraise your own knowledge and background in each area, *measured against the job sought*, and identify any areas in which you are weak. Be critical and realistic – do not flatter yourself.

4) Do some general reading in areas in which you feel you may be weak

For example, if the job involves supervision and your past experience has NOT, some general reading in supervisory methods and practices, particularly in the field of human relations, might be useful. Do NOT study agency procedures or detailed manuals. The oral board will be testing your understanding and capacity, not your memory.

5) Get a good night's sleep and watch your general health and mental attitude

You will want a clear head at the interview. Take care of a cold or any other minor ailment, and of course, no hangovers.

What should be done on the day of the interview?

Now comes the day of the interview itself. Give yourself plenty of time to get there. Plan to arrive somewhat ahead of the scheduled time, particularly if your appointment is in the fore part of the day. If a previous candidate fails to appear, the board might be ready for you a bit early. By early afternoon an oral board is almost invariably behind schedule if there are many candidates, and you may have to wait. Take along a book or magazine to read, or your application to review, but leave any extraneous material in the waiting room when you go in for your interview. In any event, relax and compose yourself.

The matter of dress is important. The board is forming impressions about you – from your experience, your manners, your attitude, and your appearance. Give your personal appearance careful attention. Dress your best, but not your flashiest. Choose conservative, appropriate clothing, and be sure it is immaculate. This is a business interview, and your appearance should indicate that you regard it as such. Besides, being well groomed and properly dressed will help boost your confidence.

Sooner or later, someone will call your name and escort you into the interview room. *This is it.* From here on you are on your own. It is too late for any more preparation. But remember, you asked for this opportunity to prove your fitness, and you are here because your request was granted.

What happens when you go in?

The usual sequence of events will be as follows: The clerk (who is often the board stenographer) will introduce you to the chairman of the oral board, who will introduce you to the other members of the board. Acknowledge the introductions before you sit down. Do not be surprised if you find a microphone facing you or a stenotypist sitting by. Oral interviews are usually recorded in the event of an appeal or other review.

Usually the chairman of the board will open the interview by reviewing the highlights of your education and work experience from your application – primarily for the benefit of the other members of the board, as well as to get the material into the record. Do not interrupt or comment unless there is an error or significant misinterpretation; if that is the case, do not hesitate. But do not quibble about insignificant matters. Also, he will usually ask you some question about your education, experience or your present job – partly to get you to start talking and to establish the interviewing "rapport." He may start the actual questioning, or turn it over to one of the other members. Frequently, each member undertakes the questioning on a particular area, one in which he is perhaps most competent, so you can expect each member to participate in the examination. Because time is limited, you may also expect some rather abrupt switches in the direction the questioning takes, so do not be upset by it. Normally, a board member will not pursue a single line of questioning unless he discovers a particular strength or weakness.

After each member has participated, the chairman will usually ask whether any member has any further questions, then will ask you if you have anything you wish to add. Unless you are expecting this question, it may floor you. Worse, it may start you off on an extended, extemporaneous speech. The board is not usually seeking more information. The question is principally to offer you a last opportunity to present further qualifications or to indicate that you have nothing to add. So, if you feel that a significant qualification or characteristic has been overlooked, it is proper to point it out in a sentence or so. Do not compliment the board on the thoroughness of their examination – they have been sketchy, and you know it. If you wish, merely say, "No thank you, I have nothing further to add." This is a point where you can "talk yourself out" of a good impression or fail to present an important bit of information. Remember, *you close the interview yourself*.

The chairman will then say, "That is all, Mr. _____, thank you." Do not be startled; the interview is over, and quicker than you think. Thank him, gather your belongings and take your leave. Save your sigh of relief for the other side of the door.

How to put your best foot forward

Throughout this entire process, you may feel that the board individually and collectively is trying to pierce your defenses, seek out your hidden weaknesses and embarrass and confuse you. Actually, this is not true. They are obliged to make an appraisal of your qualifications for the job you are seeking, and they want to see you in your best light. Remember, they must interview all candidates and a non-cooperative candidate may become a failure in spite of their best efforts to bring out his qualifications. Here are 15 suggestions that will help you:

1) Be natural – Keep your attitude confident, not cocky

If you are not confident that you can do the job, do not expect the board to be. Do not apologize for your weaknesses, try to bring out your strong points. The board is interested in a positive, not negative, presentation. Cockiness will antagonize any board member and make him wonder if you are covering up a weakness by a false show of strength.

2) Get comfortable, but don't lounge or sprawl

Sit erectly but not stiffly. A careless posture may lead the board to conclude that you are careless in other things, or at least that you are not impressed by the importance of the occasion. Either conclusion is natural, even if incorrect. Do not fuss with your clothing, a pencil or an ashtray. Your hands may occasionally be useful to emphasize a point; do not let them become a point of distraction.

3) Do not wisecrack or make small talk

This is a serious situation, and your attitude should show that you consider it as such. Further, the time of the board is limited – they do not want to waste it, and neither should you.

4) Do not exaggerate your experience or abilities

In the first place, from information in the application or other interviews and sources, the board may know more about you than you think. Secondly, you probably will not get away with it. An experienced board is rather adept at spotting such a situation, so do not take the chance.

5) If you know a board member, do not make a point of it, yet do not hide it

Certainly you are not fooling him, and probably not the other members of the board. Do not try to take advantage of your acquaintanceship – it will probably do you little good.

6) Do not dominate the interview

Let the board do that. They will give you the clues – do not assume that you have to do all the talking. Realize that the board has a number of questions to ask you, and do not try to take up all the interview time by showing off your extensive knowledge of the answer to the first one.

7) Be attentive

You only have 20 minutes or so, and you should keep your attention at its sharpest throughout. When a member is addressing a problem or question to you, give him your undivided attention. Address your reply principally to him, but do not exclude the other board members.

8) Do not interrupt

A board member may be stating a problem for you to analyze. He will ask you a question when the time comes. Let him state the problem, and wait for the question.

9) Make sure you understand the question

Do not try to answer until you are sure what the question is. If it is not clear, restate it in your own words or ask the board member to clarify it for you. However, do not haggle about minor elements.

10) Reply promptly but not hastily

A common entry on oral board rating sheets is "candidate responded readily," or "candidate hesitated in replies." Respond as promptly and quickly as you can, but do not jump to a hasty, ill-considered answer.

11) Do not be peremptory in your answers

A brief answer is proper – but do not fire your answer back. That is a losing game from your point of view. The board member can probably ask questions much faster than you can answer them.

12) Do not try to create the answer you think the board member wants

He is interested in what kind of mind you have and how it works – not in playing games. Furthermore, he can usually spot this practice and will actually grade you down on it.

13) Do not switch sides in your reply merely to agree with a board member

Frequently, a member will take a contrary position merely to draw you out and to see if you are willing and able to defend your point of view. Do not start a debate, yet do not surrender a good position. If a position is worth taking, it is worth defending.

14) Do not be afraid to admit an error in judgment if you are shown to be wrong

The board knows that you are forced to reply without any opportunity for careful consideration. Your answer may be demonstrably wrong. If so, admit it and get on with the interview.

15) Do not dwell at length on your present job

The opening question may relate to your present assignment. Answer the question but do not go into an extended discussion. You are being examined for a *new* job, not your present one. As a matter of fact, try to phrase ALL your answers in terms of the job for which you are being examined.

Basis of Rating

Probably you will forget most of these "do's" and "don'ts" when you walk into the oral interview room. Even remembering them all will not ensure you a passing grade. Perhaps you did not have the qualifications in the first place. But remembering them will help you to put your best foot forward, without treading on the toes of the board members.

Rumor and popular opinion to the contrary notwithstanding, an oral board wants you to make the best appearance possible. They know you are under pressure – but they also want to see how you respond to it as a guide to what your reaction would be under the pressures of the job you seek. They will be influenced by the degree of poise you display, the personal traits you show and the manner in which you respond.

ABOUT THIS BOOK

This book contains tests divided into Examination Sections. Go through each test, answering every question in the margin. We have also attached a sample answer sheet at the back of the book that can be removed and used. At the end of each test look at the answer key and check your answers. On the ones you got wrong, look at the right answer choice and learn. Do not fill in the answers first. Do not memorize the questions and answers, but understand the answer and principles involved. On your test, the questions will likely be different from the samples. Questions are changed and new ones added. If you understand these past questions you should have success with any changes that arise. Tests may consist of several types of questions. We have additional books on each subject should more study be advisable or necessary for you. Finally, the more you study, the better prepared you will be. This book is intended to be the last thing you study before you walk into the examination room. Prior study of relevant texts is also recommended. NLC publishes some of these in our Fundamental Series. Knowledge and good sense are important factors in passing your exam. Good luck also helps. So now study this Passbook, absorb the material contained within and take that knowledge into the examination. Then do your best to pass that exam.

EXAMINATION SECTION

EXAMINATION SECTION
TEST 1

DIRECTIONS: Each question or incomplete statement is followed by several suggested answers or completions. Select the one that BEST answers the question or completes the statement. *PRINT THE LETTER OF THE CORRECT ANSWER IN THE SPACE AT THE RIGHT.*

1. To measure the diameter of a replacement pump shaft, a(n) _____ should be used.   1._____
   - A. surveyor's chain
   - B. micrometer
   - C. metallic tape
   - D. engineer's scale

2. A _____ is used to bypass storm flow in a combined-sewerage system.   2._____
   - A. drop inlet
   - B. side weir
   - C. hydraulic jump
   - D. baffle

3. The PRIMARY element in a control system is the   3._____
   - A. transmitter
   - B. receiver
   - C. sensor
   - D. controller

4. The use of water to break down complex substances into simpler ones is called   4._____
   - A. dissolving
   - B. hydrolysis
   - C. coagulation
   - D. hydrostasis

5. In its progress through a pumping station, wastewater FIRST passes through a   5._____
   - A. comminutor
   - B. chlorine room
   - C. wet well
   - D. barminutor

6. Which of the following is NOT one of the main operational factors for a barminutor?   6._____
   - A. Amount of debris in wastewater
   - B. Number of units in service
   - C. Head loss through unit
   - D. Removal of floatables

7. Which of the following precautions must be taken before attempting to repair a surface aerator?   7._____
   - A. Shut down aerator
   - B. Drain aeration tank
   - C. Secure header assembly
   - D. Test atmosphere for toxic gases

8. Which of the following source types would MOST likely influence the pH of wastewater?   8._____
   - A. Industrial
   - B. Commercial
   - C. Agricultural
   - D. Domestic

9. Each of the following items should be carefully controlled in an activated sludge plant in order to prevent sludge bulking EXCEPT   9._____
   - A. filamentous growth
   - B. length of aeration time
   - C. return sludge rate
   - D. sludge age

10. Sludge blanket depths may be measured by the use of

    A. ultrasonic transmitters and receivers
    B. pressure gages
    C. floats connected to cables
    D. bubbler tubes

11. The vertical distance from the normal water surface to the top of the confining wall of a pond or tank is called the

    A. freeboard   B. force main
    C. header   D. stop log

12. Suspended solids in the effluent from a trickling filter plant may be caused by

    A. heavy sloughing from the filters
    B. precipitation of solids in the secondary filter
    C. condensation of effluent on secondary equipment
    D. flotation of solids in the primary clarifier

13. What is MOST often produced during the decomposition of domestic wastes?

    A. Phenols   B. Oxygen
    C. Hydrogen sulfide   D. Sulfur

14. Air compressor vibration sensing devices are used to measure each of the following EXCEPT

    A. flow   B. velocity
    C. acceleration   D. displacement

15. The height or energy of liquids above a certain point is measured in terms of

    A. discharge rate   B. volume
    C. flow   D. head

16. Factors in the design of sanitary sewers include each of the following EXCEPT

    A. maximum rate for an entire service area's domestic sewage within a specified time period
    B. maximum rates from commercial and industrial areas
    C. infiltration allowance for entire service area
    D. maximum rates from domestic and industrial/commercial sources combined

17. Which of the following could prevent a pump from starting?

    A. Tripped circuit breakers
    B. Air leaks in suction line
    C. High discharge head
    D. Lack of priming

18. Through which stage would wastewater undergoing chemical-physical treatment pass FIRST?

    A. Precipitation   B. Stripping
    C. Flocculation   D. Slaking

19. Which of the following could be considered a normal operating condition for micro-screens?   19.____

    A. High flow   B. High pH level
    C. Low pH flow   D. Toxic wastes

20. The tank in which sludges are placed in order to allow decomposition is known as the   20.____

    A. emulsion   B. dessicator
    C. digester   D. percolator

21. The conversion of large solid sludge particles into fine particles that can be dissolved or suspended in water is called   21.____

    A. hydrolysis   B. liquefaction
    C. comminution   D. recirculation

22. A mixture in which two or more liquid substances are held in suspension is called a(n)   22.____

    A. solution   B. electrolyte
    C. emulsion   D. reagent

23. What is the term for a mass of sludge containing a highly concentrated population of microorganisms?   23.____

    A. Septic   B. Seed
    C. Shock load   D. Slug

24. Which of the following forms of nitrogen is LEAST important to the wastewater treatment process?   24.____

    A. Nitrate   B. Ammonia   C. Elemental   D. Organic

25. What is the term for water leaving a centrifuge after the removal of most solids?   25.____

    A. Cation exchange   B. Centration
    C. Flocculation   D. Turbidity

KEY (CORRECT ANSWERS)

1. B
2. B
3. C
4. B
5. C

6. D
7. A
8. A
9. D
10. A

11. A
12. A
13. C
14. A
15. D

16. D
17. A
18. C
19. D
20. C

21. B
22. C
23. B
24. C
25. B

TEST 2

DIRECTIONS: Each question or incomplete statement is followed by several suggested answers or completions. Select the one that BEST answers the question or completes the statement. *PRINT THE LETTER OF THE CORRECT ANSWER IN THE SPACE AT THE RIGHT.*

1. The MOST effective treatment process for destroying or removing bacteria from waste-water is through

   A. activated sludge process
   B. trickling filter
   C. chlorination
   D. sedimentation

   1.____

2. Which of the following tasks is NOT associated with the starting of a comminutor?

   A. Check positioning of inlet and outlet gases
   B. Inspect for frayed cables
   C. Adjust cutter blades
   D. Inspect for lubrication and oil leaks

   2.____

3. One of the objectives of digester mixing is

   A. the use of waste gas to run mixers
   B. adequate cooling throughout digester contents
   C. the release of hydrogen sulfide gas
   D. microorganic inoculation of raw sludge

   3.____

4. Which type of bacteria would give the STRONGEST indication of the possible presence of pathogenic bacteria in waste-water?

   A. Coliform   B. Filamentous
   C. Heterotrophic   D. Facultative

   4.____

5. Cryogenic oxygen plants should be shut down for maintenance every

   A. six months   B. year
   C. two years   D. five years

   5.____

6. At the _____ stage in the biological treatment process, aerobic bacteria uses dissolved oxygen to convert carbon compounds to carbon dioxide.

   A. clarifying   B. carbonaceous
   C. nitrification   D. coagulation

   6.____

7. _____ is NOT an influential factor in the settleability of solids in a clarifier.

   A. Detention time
   B. Flow velocity
   C. The movement of sludge scrapers
   D. Temperature

   7.____

5

8. Which concentration of total organic carbon, in milligrams per liter, would be considered *moderate* in wastewater?

   A. 50   B. 100   C. 200   D. 300

9. Which of the following is a volume reduction alternative in sludge processing?

   A. Centrifugation
   B. Chemical conditioning
   C. Flotation
   D. Drying

10. The hydraulic loading for a phosphate stripper depends on the

    A. dissolved oxygen of the activated sludge
    B. pH of wastewater
    C. BOD loading of the unit
    D. ability of the aerobic phosphate stripper to remain aerobic

11. The range of typical carrying capacities, in gallons per minute, of package-plant pumping stations is

    A. less than 600
    B. 200-700
    C. 100-1,600
    D. 700-10,000

12. When a sludge becomes too light and refuses to settle properly in a clarifier, this is known as

    A. centration
    B. precipitation
    C. comminution
    D. bulking

13. In a wet well, level control systems include each of the following EXCEPT

    A. bubblers   B. hearts   C. floats   D. electrodes

14. Which of the following is NOT one of the primary sources of odors in a wastewater treatment plant?

    A. Unwashed grit
    B. The carbon adsorption process
    C. Sludge incinerators
    D. Waste-gas burning

15. A chemical property used in the classification of irrigation waters is

    A. pH
    B. total dissolved solids
    C. BOD
    D. aeration

16. Which of the following is NOT a potential use for the dissolved air flotation process?

    A. Solids recovery
    B. Coagulation
    C. Wastewater treatment
    D. Water recovery

17. Each of the following is a principal factor determining the use of pumping stations in sewage collection EXCEPT the

    A. elevation of the area or district to be serviced
    B. location of natural drainage areas in relation to the service area
    C. cost of a pumping station
    D. cost of trunk sewer construction

18. Through which stage would wastewater undergoing chemical-physical treatment pass LAST?

    A. Carbon adsorption
    B. Lime recovery
    C. Flocculation
    D. Slaking

19. Which of the following practices is NOT included in the maintenance of equipment in package operation plants?

    A. Changing oil in the speed reducer
    B. Adjusting aeration equipment
    C. Washing tank walls and channels
    D. Inspecting the air-lift pump

20. What chemical solution is capable of neutralizing acids or bases without greatly altering pH?
    A(n)

    A. blank
    B. alkaline
    C. buffer
    D. digester

21. Which of the following types of pumps is a displacement pump?

    A. Centrifugal
    B. Electromagnetic
    C. Peripheral
    D. Diaphragm

22. A sludge whose solid portion can be separated from the liquid is referred to as

    A. anhydrous
    B. soluble
    C. hydrolytic
    D. dewaterable

23. Which of the following could indicate that a high organic waste load has reached the activated sludge process?
    A(n)

    A. *increase* in DO residual in the aeration tank
    B. *increase* in turbidity in the effluent from the secondary chamber
    C. *decrease* in nutrients in the effluent from the secondary chamber
    D. *decrease* in aeration

24. The term for the clogging of the filtering medium or a microscreen or a vacuum filter is

    A. corrosion
    B. head loss
    C. coagulation
    D. blinding

25. Through which stage in an activated sludge treatment plant would wastewater pass LAST?

    A. Grit chamber
    B. Chlorine contact chamber
    C. Settling tanks
    D. Trickling filters

KEY (CORRECT ANSWERS)

1. C
2. B
3. D
4. A
5. B

6. B
7. C
8. C
9. D
10. A

11. B
12. D
13. B
14. B
15. B

16. B
17. C
18. A
19. A
20. C

21. D
22. D
23. B
24. D
25. B

EXAMINATION SECTION
TEST 1

DIRECTIONS: Each question or incomplete statement is followed by several suggested answers or completions. Select the one that BEST answers the question or completes the statement. *PRINT THE LETTER OF THE CORRECT ANSWER IN THE SPACE AT THE RIGHT.*

1. To check for the entrance of toxic wastes into a treatment plant, each of the following may be reliably observed as indicators EXCEPT

    A. changes in color of incoming wastewater
    B. waste recording equipment
    C. odors
    D. bulking of sludge in the clarifier

    1._____

2. An increase in _____ could cause a demand for more oxygen in an aeration tank.

    A. inert or inorganic wastes
    B. pH
    C. toxic substances
    D. microorganisms

    2._____

3. Chlorine may be added for hydrogen sulfide control in the

    A. collection lines   B. aeration tank
    C. plant effluent   D. trickling filter

    3._____

4. The range of typical carrying capacities, in gallons per minute, of intermediate pumping stations is

    A. less than 600   B. 200-700
    C. 100-1,600   D. 700-10,000

    4._____

5. A low sulfanator injector vacuum reading could be caused by

    A. missing gasket
    B. high back pressure
    C. high-volume injector flow
    D. wrong orifice

    5._____

6. Before starting a rotating biological contactor process, each of the following should be checked EXCEPT

    A. lubrication   B. biomass
    C. clearance   D. tightness

    6._____

7. The capacity for water or wastewater to neutralize acids is expressed in terms of

    A. pH   B. oxygen demand
    C. alkalinity   D. acidity

    7._____

8. Which of the following is NOT one of the available methods for determining stormwater flow for the purpose of storm sewer design?

    8._____

9

A. Rainfall and runoff correlation studies
B. Inlet method
C. Hydrograph method
D. Outlet method

9. What is the term for the accumulation of residue that appears on trickling filters and must be removed periodically?

   A. Sludges   B. Slurries   C. Slugs   D. Sloughings

10. A sludge containing a high number of living organisms is referred to as

    A. raw   B. activated   C. primary   D. toxic

11. Which of the following is NOT a plant location where liquid mixing is commonly practiced?

    A. Ponds
    B. Hydraulic jumps in open channels
    C. Pipelines
    D. Venturi flumes

12. Which of the following industries releases primarily inorganic wastes in its effluent?

    A. Paper
    C. Gravel washing
    B. Petroleum
    D. Dairy

13. Which of the following collection system variables could upset a plant's activated sludge process?

    A. Discharge by industrial cleaning operations
    B. Chlorination of return sludge flows
    C. Decreases in influent flows
    D. Recycling of digester supernatant

14. The second-stage BOD is also referred to as the _____ stage.

    A. carbonaceous
    C. flocculation
    B. pretreatment
    D. nitrification

15. When organic matter decomposes to form foul-smelling products associated with the lack of free oxygen, this condition is known as

    A. shock loading
    C. sloughing
    B. septicity
    D. sidestreaming

16. Which type of bacteria has the HIGHEST optimum temperature for treatment?

    A. Mesophilic
    C. Thermophilic
    B. Cryophilic
    D. Psychrophilic

17. The COD test

    A. estimates the total oxygen consumed
    B. measures the carbon oxygen demand
    C. provides results more quickly than the BOD test
    D. measures only the nitrification oxygen demand

18. Which of the following is NOT considered a major factor that may cause variations in lab test results? 18._____

    A. The nature of the material being examined
    B. Testing equipment
    C. Sampling procedures
    D. The quantity of material being examined

19. The treatment process that MOST effectively removes suspended solids from wastewater is 19._____

    A. sedimentation B. flocculation
    C. skimming D. comminution

20. Which of the following is a thickening alternative in sludge processing? 20._____

    A. Flotation B. Incineration
    C. Elutriation D. Wet oxidation

21. The device that continuously adds the flow of wastewater into a plant is the 21._____

    A. aggregate B. turbidity meter
    C. titrator D. totalizer

22. Two types of measurement required in connection with the operation of a treatment plant are 22._____

    A. effluent and downstream
    B. temperature and dissolved oxygen
    C. in-plant and receiving water
    D. temperature and receiving water

23. You may NOT dispose of excess activated sludge waste from package plants 23._____

    A. at a nearby treatment plant
    B. by anaerobic digestion
    C. by removal by septic tank pumper
    D. by aeration in a holding tank, then deposit in a sanitary landfill

24. What is the term for the combination of activated sludge with raw wastewater in a treatment plant? 24._____

    A. Median B. Liquefaction
    C. Effluent D. Mixed liquor

25. Landfills produce poisonous _____ gas as a byproduct of decomposition. 25._____

    A. methane B. nitrogen
    C. chlorofluorocarbons D. argon

KEY (CORRECT ANSWERS)

1. B
2. D
3. A
4. D
5. B

6. B
7. C
8. D
9. D
10. B

11. A
12. C
13. A
14. D
15. B

16. C
17. C
18. D
19. B
20. A

21. D
22. C
23. B
24. D
25. A

———

TEST 2

DIRECTIONS: Each question or incomplete statement is followed by several suggested answers or completions. Select the one that BEST answers the question or completes the statement. *PRINT THE LETTER OF THE CORRECT ANSWER IN THE SPACE AT THE RIGHT.*

1. Which of the following types of pumps is a kinetic pump?   1.____

    A. Rotary
    B. Piston plunger
    C. Hydraulic ram
    D. Blow case

2. What device is used to keep floated solids out of the effluent in dissolved air flotation thickeners?   2.____

    A. Cloth screens
    B. Microscreens
    C. Effluent baffles
    D. Water sprays

3. The _____ is NOT one of the primary factors affecting the flow of wastewater and sewage in sewers.   3.____

    A. viscosity of the liquid
    B. cross-sectional area of the system conduit
    C. time of day
    D. pipe surface

4. What is the term for washing a digested sludge in the plant effluent?   4.____

    A. Masking
    B. Elutriation
    C. Hydrolysis
    D. Slaking

5. _____ is NOT an objective in periodically pumping sludge from the primary clarifier to the digester.   5.____

    A. Prevention of pump clogging
    B. Prevention of digester overload
    C. Allowance for thicker sludge pumping
    D. Maintenance of good clarifier conditions

6. The toxic chemical LEAST likely to be encountered by treatment plant operators is(are)   6.____

    A. mercury
    B. acids
    C. fluorocarbons
    D. bases

7. Which concentration of total dissolved solids, in milligrams per liter, would be the MINIMUM required in order to be considered *strong* in wastewater?   7.____

    A. 250   B. 500   C. 850   D. 1,200

8. What is the term for the treatment process in which a tank or reactor is filled, the water is treated, and the tank is emptied?   8.____

    A. Flocculation
    B. Centration
    C. Batch process
    D. Pond process

9. The mixing of a compound with water to produce a true chemical reaction is to   9.____

    A. dissolve   B. slake   C. strip   D. hydrate

13

10. If the difference in elevation between inflow and outflow sewers is greater than 1.5 feet, which device is needed?

    A. Side weir
    B. Drop inlet
    C. Baffles
    D. Inlet casting

11. Intermittent releases or discharges of industrial wastes are known as

    A. slurries
    B. slugs
    C. splashes
    D. stop logs

12. Results from the settleability test of activated sludge solids may be used to

    A. calculate BOD
    B. determine probable flow rates at which sludges may clog equipment
    C. calculate sludge age
    D. determine ability of solids to separate from liquid in final clarifier

13. The device used to measure the temperature of an effluent is a

    A. thermometer
    B. Bourdon tube
    C. thermocouple
    D. pug mill

14. Which source is typically the HEAVIEST contributor of total solids in a service area's wastewater supply?

    A. Industrial wastes
    B. Domestic wash waters
    C. Storm runoff
    D. Human biological wastes

15. The term for liquid removed from a settled sludge is

    A. hydrolyte
    B. supernatant
    C. aliquot
    D. slurry

16. A unit of wastewater moving through the treatment system without dispersing or mixing with the rest of the wastewater in the system is called

    A. centration
    B. plug flow
    C. putrefaction
    D. slugging

17. What is the term for the groups or clumps of bacteria or particles that have clustered together during the treatment process?

    A. Coagulants
    B. Slurries
    C. Flocs
    D. Slugs

18. The purpose of PRIMARY sedimentation is to remove

    A. settleable and floatable material
    B. roots, rags, and large debris
    C. suspended and dissolved solids
    D. sand and gravel

19. _____ would NOT cause an increase in effluent coliform levels at a treatment plant.

    A. Mixing problems
    B. An increase in effluent BOD
    C. Solids accumulation in the contact chamber
    D. High chlorine residual

20. What is the term used to describe bacteria that can live under either aerobic or anaerobic conditions?　20.____

    A. Cultured
    B. Agglomerated
    C. Filamentous
    D. Facultative

21. Which devices are NOT used during pretreatment?　21.____

    A. Racks
    B. Comminutors
    C. Screens
    D. Coagulators

22. Through which stage in an activated sludge treatment plant would wastewater pass FIRST?　22.____

    A. Grit chambers
    B. Bar racks
    C. Settling tanks
    D. Primary sedimentation

23. The inorganic gas LEAST likely to be found around a treatment plant is　23.____

    A. ammonia
    B. methane
    C. hydrogen sulfide
    D. mercaptans

24. The soils in an effluent disposal on land program may be tested using each of the following procedures EXCEPT　24.____

    A. BOD
    B. conductivity
    C. pH
    D. cation exchange capacity

25. Which of the following is a conditioning alternative in sludge processing?　25.____

    A. Centrifugation
    B. Drying
    C. Composing
    D. Elutriation

KEY (CORRECT ANSWERS)

1. C		11. B
2. C		12. D
3. C		13. C
4. B		14. A
5. A		15. B
6. C		16. B
7. C		17. C
8. C		18. A
9. B		19. D
10. B		20. D

21. D
22. B
23. D
24. A
25. D

EXAMINATION SECTION
TEST 1

DIRECTIONS: Answer the following questions directly, briefly, and succinctly.

Questions 1-10.

DIRECTIONS: What is the purpose of each of the following pieces of equipment in sewage treatment?

1. Coarse racks
2. Fine bar screens
3. Fine screens
4. Screening grinders
5. Grit chambers
6. Grit washers
7. Settling tanks
8. Aeration tanks
9. Sludge digesters
10. Sluice gates or weirs

Questions 11-20.

DIRECTIONS: What are the chief causes for each of the following pieces of equipment becoming defective? For each cause, indicate how you would repair the defect.

11. Mechanical screens
12. Screening grinders
13. Grit collectors
14. Grit washers
15. Main sewage and circulating pumps
16. Sludge pumps
17. Settling tanks
18. Aeration tanks
19. Sluice gates
20. Storage tanks

Questions 21-25.

21. What safety precaution should you take when making repairs on electric equipment?
22. What safety precaution should you take when making repairs on a mechanical rack?
23. What safety precaution should you take when grinding tools?
24. What safety precaution should you take when working with digester gas?
25. What safety precaution should you take when handling a leaking chlorine cylinder?

Questions 26-30.

26. How is grit removed from grit channels?
27. What should be done to protect flocculator mechanism in case of accumulation of grit and sand in the flocculators?
28. What is the usual period of detention in settling tanks?
29. Indicate, on a simple sketch, the direction of flow in settling tanks in use in the city.
30. What must be done in order to prevent digestion of sludge in settling tanks?

Questions 31-35.

31. In chemical precipitation, in what form are chemicals received for mixing with the sewage to increase settling?
32. In the activated sludge process, what is mixed with the raw or clarified sewage?
33. Where, in the activated sludge process, are diffuser blocks used?
34. Why is chlorine added to effluent discharging from some sewage treatment plants into bodies of water?
35. How are sludge digestion tanks heated?

Questions 36-40.

36. What is the average period of sludge detention in primary tanks?
37. What happens to sludge volume in secondary tanks?
38. What is usually done with the digested sludge resulting from plant operation?
39. What use is made of skimmings from settling tanks?
40. At what point in the activated sludge process is the sample for checking residual oxygen taken?

Questions 41-45.

41. For what is a venturi motor used?
42. What type of pump is generally used for pumping raw sewage?

43. What type of pump is generally used for pumping sludge?

44. How should electric motors be cleaned?

45. What type of fire extinguisher should be used for fires on electrical equipment?

Questions 46-50.

46. Assume that you are pumping water into a tank at the rate of 200 gallons per minute and that you are withdrawing water at the rate of 75 gallons per minute. How long will it take to add 60,000 gallons of water to the tank?

47.

The figures above show two readings of a watt-hour meter taken twenty-four hours apart. How many k.w. hours were used in that period?

4 (#1)

KEY (CORRECT ANSWERS)

1. Remove coarse materials – cans, ashes, rags, timber, etc.

2. Remove smaller materials that go through coarse racks

3. Remove particles of sewage and fine floating material (screens also protect equipment of plant through which sewage must pass)

4. Reduce size of removed particles

5. Catch sand, gravel, ashes, and other gritty material

6. Remove odor-producing materials from the grit

7. Settle out materials in sewage (sludge)

8. Treat sewage by application of air

9. Digest sludge and produce gas

10. Control and measure flow of sewage

11. Overloading causes breakage of cables, chains, shear pins. Repair by removing cause of overload and replacing broken part.

12. Overloading through delivery of too much material or dulling of knives. Repair by opening grinder, removing obstructing material, and replacing or reversing knives.

13. Moving parts – chains, shoes, pins, sprockets, flights – becoming worn. Repair by replacing worn parts.

14. Clogging of slide valves. Repair by cleaning and replacing pipe fittings. Clean, repair, and adjust such parts as chains and diaphragms.

15. Motor failure. Report to plant engineer. Loss of prime and leakage. Adjust or replace packing, adjust water seal, and reprime.

16. Obstruction under valves, over-load, slogging or leaks. Repair by replacing faulty gaskets and worn packing for air leaks, to remove obstructions, take off valve covers, and clean.

17. Same as 13

18. Plates or valves becoming clogged or broken. Service valves, clean and replace clogged or broken plates.

19. Gate skewed or jammed, spindle bent, gears jammed or broken. Re-adjust or replace.

20. Same as 14.

21. Make sure power is off and equipment grounded

22. Make sure equipment cannot be set in motion

23. Wear goggles

5 (#1)

24. Use proper mask, keep flame away

25. Wear special gas mask and rubber gloves

26. Longitudinal or revolving scrapers

27. Periodic flushing

28. One to two hours

29.

30. Continuous removal of settled sludge

31. Powder, dry with chlorine

32. Biologically active sludge, air (1/2)

33. Base of aeration tanks

34. Reduces harmful bacteria, minimizes disagreeable odors

35. Heat provided by circulating warm water through coils in the tanks

36. 20 days approximately for primary digestion tanks or 2 hours for primary settling tanks

37. Compacted to about 50% of original volume

38. Dumped at sea or used as landfill

39. Sold as fat

40. Between aeration tank and secondary settlement tank or at outlet of secondary settling tank

41. Measure flow of water

42. Centrifugal pump

43. Piston or reciprocating pump

44. Carbon tetrachloride, compressed air, rags (not waste)

45. CO_2, fire foam, carbon tetrachloride

46. 8 hours

47. 6583   or   6583
     4128   4129
     ----   ----
     2455   or   2454

EXAMINATION SECTION
TEST 1

DIRECTIONS: Each question or incomplete statement is followed by several suggested answers or completions. Select the one that BEST answers the question or completes the statement. *PRINT THE LETTER OF THE CORRECT ANSWER IN THE SPACE AT THE RIGHT.*

1. The rate at which solids settle out of sewage in a sedimentation tank is dependent MAINLY on the

    A. depth of sewage in tank
    B. velocity of flow through tank
    C. water pressure
    D. amount of solids in sewage

2. Flow of sewage to the treatment plant from the intercepting sewer is controlled by a

    A. sluice gate   B. flight
    C. reduction valve   D. bar screen

3. The process of adding chemicals to the sewage to increase the rate of settlement of suspended solids is known as

    A. calcination   B. oxydation
    C. flocculation   D. chlorination

4. Large objects, such as sticks, are removed from raw sewage by a

    A. sludge pump   B. settling tank
    C. bar rack   D. ejector

5. Grit is MOST frequently moved from the grit chamber to the grit storage tank by

    A. gravity flow   B. compressed air
    C. wheelbarrow   D. conveyor belt

6. The porous plates through which air enters the aeration chamber in the activates sludge process are known as

    A. diffusers   B. nozzles
    C. oxygen lances   D. pressure plates

7. The *strength* of sewage is measured by determining its

    A. M.D.   B. HP   C. G.P.M.   D. B.O.D.

8. In order to prevent digestion of sludge in sedimentation tanks, the sludge is

    A. chemically treated   B. aerated
    C. continuously removed   D. heated

9. One of the chemicals used to increase the rate of settling of suspended solids in sewage is

    A. bromine   B. carbon   C. copper   D. fluorine

10. Chlorine is added to sewage to
    A. aid sludge digestion
    B. kill bacteria
    C. increase B.T.U. content of gas
    D. dewater sludge in storage tanks

11. A sewer which receives BOTH rain water and sewage from residences is known as a _____ sewer.
    A. storm   B. sanitary   C. regulated   D. combined

12. Treated sewage flowing out of the sewage treatment plant is known as the
    A. desiccant   B. decanter   C. effluent   D. waste

13. In the aerated sludge process, grease can conveniently be removed from the sewage in the
    A. wet well
    B. final sedimentation chamber
    C. grit chamber
    D. screening chamber

14. A device used to control the rate of flow of sewage is known as a
    A. weir   B. penstock   C. agitator   D. stator

15. A venturi meter is used to measure _____ of sewage.
    A. pressure   B. temperature
    C. flow   D. depth

16. Sludge gas is composed MAINLY of
    A. methane   B. carbon monoxide
    C. hydrogen sulfide   D. ammonia

17. Overloads on reciprocating pumps can be prevented by _____ valves.
    A. check   B. relief   C. gate   D. globe

18. A valve that permits flow in only one direction is a _____ valve.
    A. check   B. plug   C. gate   D. globe

19. Where a quick closing action is desired, the type of valve that should be used is a(n)
    A. globe   B. needle   C. gate   D. angle

20. The one of the following types of valves that causes the LEAST resistance to the flow of sewage is a(n)
    A. globe   B. angle   C. gate   D. key

21. Cavitation (pitting) in centrifugal pumps would MOST probably occur in the
    A. packing glands   B. roller bearings
    C. pump impellers   D. shaft

22. The type of pump MOST commonly used to pump sludge is the

    A. turbine
    B. centrifugal
    C. volute
    D. reciprocating

23. If the bearings on a large pump become excessively hot, the BEST thing to do is to

    A. pour cold water on the bearings to cool them
    B. fill the oil cup and slow the pump till the bearings cool
    C. stop the motor and check the condition of the bearings and oil or grease
    D. shunt the suction and discharge valves till the pump cools, then reopen valves slowly

24. Priming is MOST frequently required in a _____ pump.

    A. centrifugal
    B. reciprocating
    C. rotary
    D. gear

25. When gland nuts on a sewage pump are properly tightened,

    A. there will be slight leakage through the packing
    B. the packing is not compressed
    C. the lantern will rotate
    D. the stuffing box cannot overheat

KEY (CORRECT ANSWERS)

1.	B	11.	D
2.	A	12.	C
3.	C	13.	B
4.	C	14.	A
5.	B	15.	C
6.	A	16.	A
7.	D	17.	B
8.	C	18.	A
9.	C	19.	C
10.	B	20.	C

21.	C
22.	D
23.	C
24.	A
25.	A

TEST 2

DIRECTIONS: Each question or incomplete statement is followed by several suggested answers or completions. Select the one that BEST answers the question or completes the statement. *PRINT THE LETTER OF THE CORRECT ANSWER IN THE SPACE AT THE RIGHT.*

1. The rated capacity of a pump is usually given in terms of

    A. horsepower and velocity of flow
    B. gallons per minute pumped and pressure head
    C. electrical consumption and velocity of flow
    D. electrical consumption and gallons per minute pumped

    1._____

2. Sudden shutting of the discharge valve of a centrifugal pump may damage a piping system because

    A. the impellers will turn for a short period without lubrication
    B. there will be leakage past the packing
    C. pump bearings will be scored
    D. water hammer will occur

    2._____

3. The one of the following that is used on a piece of mechanical equipment to prevent overloading is a

    A. bushing   B. shear pin
    C. split ring   D. yoke

    3._____

4. Sewage has suddenly stopped flowing from a centrifugal pump which has been working well.
   The MOST probable cause for this is that

    A. air is leaking into suction line
    B. the bearings are worn
    C. the speed of pump is excessive
    D. the oil level is inadequate

    4._____

5. The MOST viscous of the following lubricants is

    A. diesel oil   B. cup grease
    C. S.A.E. 40 oil   D. kerosene

    5._____

6. The BEST method of lubricating roller bearings if by means of

    A. light machine oil B. instrument oil
    C. diesel oil   D. grease

    6._____

7. A pipe reducer would be used to

    A. permit drawing of low pressure gas from high pressure pipes
    B. connect two lines of different sizes
    C. compress packing in a line expansion joint
    D. remove excess water from sludge lines

    7._____

8. The one of the following that is NOT a standard pipe fitting is a   8.____

   A. union   B. tap   C. tee   D. cross

9. Water hammer can be reduced by using a(n)   9.____

   A. quick closing valve   B. air chamber
   C. flanged connection   D. automatic primer

10. To be watertight, the faces of a flanged connection should be   10.____

    A. machined
    B. packed with waste
    C. coated with rubber cement
    D. etched

11. When tightening bolts on a flanged connection, the PROPER procedure is to   11.____

    A. take up each bolt wrench hard before beginning to tighten next adjacent bolt
    B. first take up one bolt wrench hard, then tighten diagonally opposite bolt wrench hard
    C. take up each bolt gradually, tightening adjacent bolts in order
    D. take up each bolt gradually, first tightening one bolt slightly, then the diagonally opposite bolt in a like manner

12. The kind of wrench used to tighten pipe would be a(n)   12.____

    A. crescent   B. open end   C. monkey   D. Stillson

13. The one of the following fire extinguisher types that should be used on a fire in an electric motor is   13.____

    A. carbon dioxide   B. soda acid
    C. water fog   D. foam

14. A safety device used to protect electrical circuits from overloads is a(n)   14.____

    A. solenoid   B. powerstat
    C. circuit breaker   D. transformer

15. The one of the following that is the MOST common reason for noisy operation of electric motors is   15.____

    A. shorted windings   B. worn brushes
    C. worn bearings   D. overloading

16. The unit of measurement used for determining the amount of energy consumed in running a motor is   16.____

    A. volt-amperes   B. kilowatt hours
    C. horsepower   D. frequency-cycle

17. The one of the following parts of an electric motor that will wear out MOST frequently is(are) the   17.____

    A. armature   B. field pieces
    C. shaft   D. brushes

18. The MOST important reason for using a fuse in an electrical circuit is to prevent excessive   18.____

    A. voltage   B. current
    C. frequency   D. resistance

19. An electrical device used to increase line voltage is a(n)   19.____

    A. alternator   B. magneto
    C. transformer   D. choke

20. The minimum size wire that should be used to supply power to a 1 H.P. motor is   20.____

    A. #14   B. #16   C. #18   D. #20

21. The one of the following that should be used to clean a commit at or is   21.____

    A. sandpaper   B. emery paper
    C. pumice   D. emery cloth

22. To clean armature windings on a motor, one should use   22.____

    A. calcium chloride   B. sodium chloride
    C. carbon tetrachloride   D. sodium hypochlorite

23. When starting an electrically driven centrifugal pump, the starting load can be reduced by   23.____

    A. opening the suction and discharge valves
    B. opening the suction valve and closing the discharge valves
    C. closing the suction and discharge valves
    D. closing the suction valve and opening the discharge valves

24. For increased safety, the frame of an electric motor should be   24.____

    A. grounded   B. shorted   C. shunted   D. painted

25. The one of the following materials that is MOST suitable for piping corrosive sludge gas is   25.____

    A. copper   B. steel   C. aluminum   D. transite

KEY (CORRECT ANSWERS)

1.	B	11.	D
2.	D	12.	D
3.	B	13.	A
4.	A	14.	C
5.	B	15.	C
6.	D	16.	B
7.	B	17.	D
8.	B	18.	B
9.	B	19.	C
10.	A	20.	A

21. A
22. C
23. B
24. A
25. D

EXAMINATION SECTION
TEST 1

DIRECTIONS: Each question or incomplete statement is followed by several suggested answers or completions. Select the one that BEST answers the question or completes the statement. *PRINT THE LETTER OF THE CORRECT ANSWER IN THE SPACE AT THE RIGHT.*

1. Assume that a certain file has a safe edge. This is an edge that has
   A. no teeth
   B. the teeth pointing backward
   C. the teeth pointing forward
   D. fine criss-cross teeth

2. The one of the following which is the proper tool for threading a round rod is a
   A. tap   B. countersink   C. counterbore   D. die

3. A rasp is a
   A. type of chisel
   B. type of file cleaner
   C. type of coarse file
   D. kind of plane

4. The one of the following which is the proper tool to use to tighten a round nut which has a series of notches cut in its outer surface is a(n) _____ wrench.
   A. box   B. spanner   C. Stillson   D. monkey

5. Small leaks resulting from poor threads on steel or wrought-iron water pipes will often stop because the leaky threads are in time filled with
   A. sediment   B. stalactite   C. rust   D. soapstone

6. A metal that can be rolled or beaten into very fine sheets is said to be
   A. anodized   B. malleable   C. tempered   D. ferrous

7. To *rod* a sewer pipe means MOST likely to
   A. clean it out by means of rods
   B. keep the pipe clear of debris by placing a grating of rods at the intake
   C. support the sewer pipe with horizontal reinforcing metal rods
   D. shore up the pipe

8. Of the following abrasives, the one which is the LEAST coarse is
   A. No. 2 emery cloth
   B. crocus cloth
   C. No. 1 sandpaper
   D. No. 1/0 sandpaper

9. In order to permit free passage of water in one direction only and prevent a reversal of flow in the pipe, it is necessary to use a _____ valve.
   A. gate   B. check   C. globe   D. needle

10. Assume that a cubic foot of water contains 7 1/2 gallons. The number of gallons of water which could be contained in a rectangular tank 3 feet long, 2 feet wide, and 2 feet deep is MOST NEARLY
    A. 12   B. 45   C. 90   D. 120

11. The weight, in pounds, of a cubic foot of fresh water is MOST NEARLY
    A. 8.5 B. 32.4 C. 62.4 D. 98.6

12. The total weight, in pounds, of ten bags of Portland cement is MOST NEARLY _____ pounds.
    A. 108 B. 187 C. 940 D. 1,200

13. If a concrete mix is said to be 1:2:4, this would mean that the mix is made up of 1 part by 1
    A. volume of cement to 2 parts by volume of sand to 4 parts by volume of coarse aggregate
    B. volume of cement to 2 parts by volume of coarse aggregate to 4 parts by volume of sand
    C. volume of coarse aggregate to 2 parts by volume of sand to 4 parts by volume of cement
    D. weight of cement to 2 parts by weight of coarse aggregate to 4 parts by weight of sand

14. The ratio of the weight of a substance to the weight of an equal volume of water is called the _____ of the substance.
    A. specific volume
    B. specific gravity
    C. viscosity
    D. fractional weight

15. Of the following, the pipe fitting which has four openings which permits connecting a line at right angles to another line is called a(n)
    A. side outlet street L
    B. double elbow
    C. tee
    D. cross

16. To tighten a nut where only a short swing of the wrench handle is possible, it is BEST to use a _____ wrench.
    A. ratchet
    B. hook spanner
    C. Stillson
    D. Bristo

17. Of the following, the proper tool to use to remove the burr from the inside of a pipe is a
    A. half round file
    B. reamer
    C. mandrel
    D. chisel

18. Fittings commonly used with copper pipe should be made of
    A. brass
    B. cast iron
    C. malleable iron
    D. pure tin

19. With respect to pipe, the abbreviation I.P.S. means
    A. Internal Pipe Size
    B. Iron Pipe Size
    C. Iron Pipe Shape
    D. International Pipe Size

20. A Stillson wrench is the proper wrench to use when tightening a

    A. square nut
    B. hexagonal nut
    C. valve gland nut
    D. pipe fitting

21. The one of the following which is the proper tool to use for cutting wood along the grain is a _____ saw.

    A. rip B. panel C. cross-cut D. back

22. The one of the following which is the proper tool to use to cut internal screw threads is a

    A. broach B. die C. tap D. stock

23. A center punch is the proper tool used to

    A. cut out the center of a gasket
    B. dent metal prior to drilling
    C. drive nails beneath the surface of the wood
    D. punch a small hole in sheet metal

24. The one of the following knots which can be safely used for tying together the ends of two dry ropes of the same size is a

    A. granny knot
    B. clove hitch
    C. half hitch
    D. square knot

25. The PRIMARY purpose of a trap under a plumbing fixture is to

    A. act as a seal against sewer gas
    B. permit cleaning out the drain line
    C. permit the recovery of valuables accidentally dropped into the fixture
    D. permit the making of tests on the drain line

26. The one of the following which contains exactly 10 board feet is a board 10 feet long, _____ inches wide, _____ inch(es) thick.

    A. 24; 1 B. 12; 2 C. 12; 1 D. 10; 1

27. Short pieces of pipe threaded on both ends are called

    A. nipples B. couplings C. bushing D. sleeves

28. The unit of electrical capacitance is the

    A. ampere B. farad C. henry D. cycle

29. As used in the electrical industry, BX means

    A. best grade of electrical wire
    B. type B extension wire
    C. metal greenfield
    D. insulated wires in flexible metal tubing

Questions 30-33.

DIRECTIONS: Questions 30 to 33, inclusive, are to be answered in accordance with the following paragraph.

One of the categories of nuisance is a chemical one and relates to the dissolved oxygen of the watercourse. The presence in sewage and industrial wastes of materials capable of undergoing biochemical oxidation and resulting in reduction of oxygen in the watercourse leads to a partial or complete depletion of this oxygen. This, in turn, leads to the subsequent production of malodorous products of decomposition, to the destruction of aquatic plant life and major fish life and to conditions offensive to sight and smell.

30. The word *malodorous* as used in the above paragraph means MOST NEARLY

    A. fragrant B. fetid C. wholesome D. redolent

31. From the above paragraph, because of pollution, the amount of dissolved oxygen in the waterways is

    A. released B. multiplied C. lessened D. saturated

32. The word *categories* as used in the above paragraph means MOST NEARLY

    A. divisions B. clubs C. symbols D. products

33. The word *offensive* as used in the above paragraph means MOST NEARLY

    A. pliable
    C. deferential
    B. complaint
    D. disagreeable

34. The terminal voltage of 5 dry cells connected in a series is _____ of one(each) cell.

    A. 1/5 the voltage
    C. 5 times the voltage
    B. the same as the voltage
    D. determined by the current

35. If a 15 ampere fuse blows out and blows out again after inserting a new fuse, it is BEST to

    A. replace it with a 10 ampere fustat
    B. replace it with two 10 ampere fuses connected in series
    C. replace it with a 20 ampere fuse
    D. have the circuit checked to find the trouble

36. Ordinary soft solder is a mixture of lead and

    A. sulphur B. brass C. zinc D. tin

37. The electrolyte used in the ordinary flashlight-type dry cell is

    A. calcium chloride
    C. manganese dioxide
    B. ammonium chloride
    D. sulfuric acid

38. An electrical transformer is an electrical device used primarily to

   A. raise or lower A.C. voltages
   B. change the frequency of alternating current
   C. rectify currents from A.C. to D.C.
   D. change currents from D.C. to A.C.

39. Of the following, the MAIN reason for the grounding of electrical equipment and circuits is to

   A. save power
   B. increase the voltage
   C. protect personnel from electric shock
   D. prevent serious short circuits

40. In order to properly ground portable electric hand tools, it is USUALLY necessary to use a

   A. solenoid
   B. circuit breaker
   C. fuse
   D. three prong plug

41. The current in a simple electrical circuit can be calculated by dividing the voltage by the resistance in ohms. Assume that the resistance of a certain circuit is 60 ohms and its voltage is 120 volts, 60 cycle A.C.
   The current in this circuit will be MOST NEARLY _____ ampere(s).

   A. 1/2   B. 2   C. 1   D. 30

42. The one of the following which is the MOST common type of motor that may be used with an A.C. or D.C. source of supply is the _____ motor.

   A. shunt
   B. squirrel cage
   C. compound
   D. series

43. The electrolyte in the ordinary storage battery is

   A. nitric acid
   B. sulphuric acid
   C. manganese dioxide
   D. ammonium chloride

44. The one of the following terms which is used in expressing the rating of a storage battery is

   A. ampere-hours
   B. amperes
   C. volt-ampere
   D. watt-hours

45. The size of the SMALLEST graduation on the ordinary 6-foot folding rule is *usually*

   A. 1/8"   B. 1/16"   C. 1/32"   D. 1/64"

46. A given saw has 8 points per inch. This saw is PROBABLY a _____ saw.

   A. cross-cut   B. hack   C. veneer   D. back

47. Assume that it takes 6 men 8 days to do a certain job. Working at the same same speed, the number of days that it will take 4 men to do this job is

    A. 9   B. 10   C. 12   D. 14

48. The sum of 3 5/8 + 4 1/4 + 6 1/2 + 7 1/8 is

    A. 20 7/8   B. 21 1/4   C. 21 1/2   D. 22 1/8

49. The fraction which is equal to .0625 is

    A. 1/64   B. 3/64   C. 1/16   D. 5/8

50. The volume, in cubic feet, of a rectangular coal bin 8 ft. long by 5 ft. wide by 7 ft. high is MOST NEARLY

    A. 40   B. 56   C. 186   D. 280

KEY (CORRECT ANSWERS)

1. A	11. C	21. A	31. C	41. B
2. D	12. C	22. C	32. A	42. D
3. C	13. A	23. B	33. D	43. B
4. B	14. B	24. D	34. C	44. A
5. C	15. D	25. A	35. D	45. B
6. B	16. A	26. C	36. D	46. A
7. A	17. B	27. A	37. B	47. C
8. B	18. A	28. B	38. A	48. C
9. B	19. B	29. D	39. C	49. C
10. C	20. D	30. B	40. D	50. D

TEST 2

DIRECTIONS: Each question or incomplete statement is followed by several suggested answers or completions. Select the one that BEST answers the question or completes the statement. *PRINT THE LETTER OF THE CORRECT ANSWER IN THE SPACE AT THE RIGHT.*

Questions 1-7

DIRECTIONS: Questions 1 to 7, inclusive, are to be answered in accordance with the following information.

At sea level, the atmosphere can exert a pressure of 14.7 pounds per square inch. This pressure is capable of sustaining a column of water having a height equal to 14.7 pounds, multiplied by 2.304 (the height of water in feet which will exert one pound per square inch pressure). No pump built can produce a perfect vacuum. The atmospheric pressure exerting its force on the surface of the water from which suction is being taken forces the water up through the suction to the pump. From this, it is evident that the maximum height which a water pump of this type can lift water is determined ultimately by the atmospheric pressure. The tightness of the pump and its ability to create a vacuum also have a bearing.

1. The meaning of the word *vacuum* as used in the above article is a
   A. space entirely devoid of matter
   B. sealed tube filled with gas
   C. bottle-shaped vessel with a double wall
   D. cleaning device

2. With reference to the above article, if a pump could produce a perfect vacuum, the MAXIMUM height, in feet, that it could lift water at sea level is MOST NEARLY
   A. 33.9   B. 29.4   C. 23.3   D. 14.7

3. With reference to the above article, a column of water having a height of 4.6 feet at sea level will exert a pressure of MOST NEARLY _____ pound(s) per square inch.
   A. 3   B. 2   C. 1   D. 1/2

4. The word *atmosphere* as used in the above article means
   A. the pull of gravity
   B. perfect vacuum
   C. the whole mass of air surrounding the earth
   D. the weight of water at sea level

5. The word *bearing* as used in the above article means MOST NEARLY
   A. direction   B. connection
   C. divergence   D. convergence

6. The word *evident* as used in the above article means MOST NEARLY

   A. disconcerting   B. obscure   C. equivocal   D. manifest

7. The word *maximum* as used in the above article means MOST NEARLY

   A. best   B. median   C. adjacent   D. greatest

8. Assume that a car travels at a constant speed of 36 miles per hour. The speed of this car, in feet per second, is MOST NEARLY (one mile equals 5,280 ft.)

   A. 3   B. 24.6   C. 52.8   D. 879.8

9. If one-third of a 19-foot length of lumber is cut off, the length of the remaining piece will measure APPROXIMATELY

   A. 8'8"   B. 9'8"   C. 12'8"   D. 13'8"

10. The circumference of a circle having a diameter of 10" is MOST NEARLY _____ inches.

    A. 3.14   B. 18.72   C. 24.96   D. 31.4

11. Assume that in the purchase of paint, the seller quotes a discount of 10%. If the price per gallon is $6.35, the actual payment in dollars per gallon is MOST NEARLY

    A. $5.72   B. $5.95   C. $6.25   D. $6.50

12. On a 1" bolt that has 10 threads per inch, if the nut is turned 6 complete turns, the distance, in inches, that the nut will move along the bolt is MOST NEARLY

    A. .3   B. .6   C. .9   D. 1

13. Assume that at one end of a 6-inch horizontal line, an 8-inch vertical line is drawn at right angles to the horizontal line. The length, in inches, between the ends of the two lines is MOST NEARLY

    A. 6   B. 8   C. 10   D. 12

Questions 14-21.

DIRECTIONS: Questions 14 to 21, inclusive, are to be answered in accordance with the following information.

In his 2012 annual report to the Mayor, the Public Works Commissioner stated that the city's basic water pollution control program begun in 1996 and costing $425 million so far would be completed in five or six years at a cost of $275 million more. However, he said, the city must spend an additional $175 million more on its marginal pollution control program to protect present and proposed beaches. Under the basic program, the city will have eliminated the last major discharges of raw sewage into the harbor. Over 800 million gallons, two thirds of the city's spent water each day, is now treated at 12 plants, to which six new plants will be added, enabling the city to treat the estimated 1.8 billion gallons that will be discharged daily in 2030. The department had about $200 million worth of municipal construction under way in 2012, and completed $85.5 millions' worth.

14. According to the above, the city will add _____ new plants. 14.____

    A. 18   B. 12   C. 6   D. 4

15. The amount of municipal construction under way in 2012 was _____ million. 15.____

    A. $85.5   B. $175   C. $200   D. $425

16. It is estimated that in 2030, the city will treat daily _____ gallons. 16.____

    A. 700 million   B. 800 million
    C. 900 million   D. 1.8 billion

17. According to the above article, the total cost of the water pollution program begun in 1996 will be _____ million. 17.____

    A. $275   B. $425   C. $700   D. $815

18. According to the above article, to protect present and proposed beaches, the city must spend an additional _____ million. 18.____

    A. $175   B. $275   C. $425   D. $450

19. The above article concerns the statements of the Commissioner of Public Works in his _____ annual report to the Mayor. 19.____

    A. 1996   B. 2002   C. 2012   D. 2013

20. The word *discharged* as used in the above article means MOST NEARLY 20.____

    A. emitted   B. erased   C. refuted   D. repelled

21. The word *pollution* as used in the above article means MOST NEARLY 21.____

    A. condensation   B. purification
    C. contamination   D. distillation

22. A tool commonly used to cut off the head of a rivet is a 22.____

    A. cold chisel   B. cape chisel   C. band saw   D. file

23. A metal washer is MOST often used with a _____ screw. 23.____

    A. wood   B. lag   C. hand   D. machine

24. A good safety rule to follow is that water should NOT be used to extinguish fires in or around electrical apparatus. Of the following, the PRIMARY reason for this is that water 24.____

    A. will damage the insulation
    B. will corrode the electrical conductors
    C. may cause the circuit fuse to blow
    D. may conduct electric current and cause a shock hazard

25. One should be extremely careful to keep open flames and sparks away from storage batteries when they are being charged because the

    A. sulphate given off during this operation is highly flammable
    B. hydrogen given off during this operation is highly flammable
    C. oxygen given off during this operation is extremely flammable
    D. static electricity of the battery may cause combustion

26. A good safety rule to follow is that an electric hand tool, such as a portable electric drill, should never be lifted or carried by its service cord.
    Of the following, the PRIMARY reason for this rule is that the

    A. tool might swing and be damaged by striking some hard object
    B. cord might be pulled off its terminals and become short circuited
    C. tool may slip out of the hand as it is hard to get a good grip on a slick rubber cord
    D. rubber covering of the cord might overstretch

27. When a man is working on a 15-foot ladder with its top placed against a wall, the MAXIMUM safe distance that he may reach out to one side of the ladder is

    A. as far out as he can reach lifting one foot off the rung for balance
    B. as far out as he can reach without bending his body more than 45 from the vertical
    C. one-third the length of the ladder
    D. as far out as his arm's length

28. When NOT in use, oily waste rags should be stored in

    A. water-tight oak barrels
    B. open metal containers
    C. sealed cardboard boxes
    D. self-closing, metal containers

29. Assume that one of your co-workers has suffered an electric shock. Artificial respiration should be started on him immediately if he is

    A. unconscious and breathing
    B. conscious and in a daze
    C. unconscious and not breathing
    D. conscious and badly burned

30. Assume that the top of a 12-foot portable straight ladder is placed against a wall but is not held by a man or fastened in any way. In order to be safe, the ladder should be placed so that the distance from the wall to the foot of the ladder is

    A. not over 3 feet
    B. not over 4 feet
    C. at least 4 feet
    D. at least 5 feet

31. Of the following, the one which is an acceptable method of caring for wooden ladders is to

    A. coat the ladder with clear shellac
    B. paint the ladder with red lead followed by a second coat of the desired color
    C. paint the ladder with a coat of paint of the desired color
    D. apply a sealer coat before painting with a second coat of the desired color

32. The MOST important safety precaution to follow when using an electric drill press is to 32.____

    A. wear safety shoes
    B. drill at a slow speed
    C. use plenty of cutting oil
    D. clamp the work firmly

33. The proper method of lifting heavy objects is to stand 33.____

    A. far enough away from the load so that, with knees bent, the back is at an angle of 45, then lift by straightening the back
    B. close to the load, with feet solidly placed and slightly apart and knees bent; then lift by straightening the legs, keeping the back as nearly vertical as possible
    C. close to the load, with feet solidly placed and far apart, knees bent; then lift by straightening the legs, keeping the body at an angle of 30°
    D. far away from the load, with knees bent and the back at an angle of 45°, then lift by straightening the knees and slowly straightening the back

34. An oilstone is often made of 34.____

    A. silicon   B. carborundum   C. tungsten   D. emery

35. To draw a circle, you should use a(n) 35.____

    A. compass   B. caliper   C. awl   D. gage

36. A *mushroomed* head is a common defect of a 36.____

    A. rivet
    B. hammer
    C. chisel
    D. screwdriver

37. The tool USUALLY used to drive a lag screw is a(n) 37.____

    A. open end wrench
    B. Stillson wrench
    C. screwdriver
    D. Allen wrench

38. It is BEST to lubricate machinery 38.____

    A. whenever you feel the oil is running low
    B. only if the machinery needs it
    C. when the machine begins to vibrate
    D. on a regular schedule

39. When repairing machinery that is to be reassembled, punch marks are often placed on parts that are next to each other. 39.____
    The reason for this is to

    A. make sure you assemble the pieces in proper order
    B. make it easier to line up the parts in proper position
    C. keep count of the number of pieces that belong to this machine
    D. provide a stop so that parts cannot be assembled too tightly

Questions 40-46.

DIRECTIONS: Questions 40 to 46, inclusive, are to be answered in accordance with the following paragraph.

At 2:30 P.M. on Monday, October 25, Mr. Paul Jones, a newly appointed Sewage Treatment Worker, started on a routine inspectional tour of the settling tanks and other sewage treatment works installations of the plant to which he was assigned. At 2:33 P.M., Mr. Jones discovered a co-worker, Mr. James P. Brown, lying unconscious on the ground. Mr. Jones quickly reported the facts to his immediate superior, Mr. Jack Rota, who immediately telephoned for an ambulance. Mr. Rota then rushed to the site and placed a heavy woolen blanket over the victim. Mr. Brown was taken to the Ave. H hospital by an ambulance driven by Mr. Dave Smith, which arrived at the sewage disposal plant at 3:02 P.M. Patrolman Robert Daly, badge number 12520, had arrived before the ambulance and recorded all the details of the incident, including the statements of Mr. Jones, Mr. Rota, and Mr. Nick Nespola, a Stationary Engineer (Electric), who stated that he saw the victim when he fell to the ground.

40. The time which elapsed between the start of the sewage treatment worker's routine inspection and the arrival of the ambulance was MOST NEARLY _____ minutes. 40.____

   A. 3 B. 28 C. 29 D. 32

41. The name of the sewage treatment worker's immediate superior was 41.____

   A. James P. Brown B. Jack Rota
   C. Paul Jones D. Robert Daly

42. The name of the patrolman was 42.____

   A. James P. Brown B. Jack Rota
   C. Paul Jones D. Robert Daly

43. Referring to the above, the incident occurred on 43.____

   A. Monday, Oct. 25 B. Monday, October 26
   C. Tuesday, Oct. 25 D. Tuesday, October 26

44. The victim was found at exactly 44.____

   A. 2:30 A.M. B. 2:33 P.M. C. 2:33 A.M. D. 2:30 P.M.

45. The sewage treatment worker's name was 45.____

   A. James P. Brown B. Jack Rota
   C. Paul Jones D. Dave Smith

46. The man named Nick Nespola was the 46.____

   A. Stationary Engineer (Electric) B. patrolman
   C. victim D. ambulance driver

47. When sharpening a tool on a grindstone, the tool is often dipped in water. The MAIN reason for this is to

    A. prevent overheating of the tool
    B. lubricate the grindstone
    C. produce a sharper edge on the tool
    D. anneal the tool

47.____

48. It is BEST to use a screwdriver having a square shank

    A. when clearance is limited
    B. on sheet metal screws
    C. on small screws
    D. where a wrench is to be used to help turn the screwdriver

48.____

49. Brass liners are often placed over the jaws of a bench vise to

    A. grip the work better
    B. prevent damage to the work
    C. protect the vise
    D. make it easier to adjust the work

49.____

50. Other than the bulb, the part of a fluorescent light that must be changed MOST often as it wears is the

    A. switch   B. ballast   C. control   D. starter

50.____

KEY (CORRECT ANSWERS)

1.	A	11.	A	21.	C	31.	A	41.	B
2.	A	12.	B	22.	A	32.	D	42.	D
3.	B	13.	C	23.	D	33.	B	43.	A
4.	C	14.	C	24.	D	34.	B	44.	B
5.	B	15.	C	25.	B	35.	A	45.	C
6.	D	16.	D	26.	B	36.	C	46.	A
7.	D	17.	C	27.	D	37.	A	47.	A
8.	C	18.	A	28.	D	38.	D	48.	D
9.	C	19.	C	29.	C	39.	B	49.	B
10.	D	20.	A	30.	A	40.	D	50.	D

EXAMINATION SECTION
TEST 1

DIRECTIONS: Each question or incomplete statement is followed by several suggested answers or completions. Select the one that BEST answers the question or completes the statement. *PRINT THE LETTER OF THE CORRECT ANSWER IN THE SPACE AT THE RIGHT.*

1. The flow of sewage into the treatment plant is USUALLY controlled by a   1.____

    A. gate valve
    B. sluice gate
    C. tainter gate
    D. parshall gate

2. Regulator gates USUALLY close when the sewage in the interceptor sewer reaches a predetermined   2.____

    A. velocity
    B. pressure
    C. temperature
    D. elevation

3. A bar screen serves the same purpose as a   3.____

    A. filter
    B. grit collector
    C. trash rack
    D. sluice gate

4. Material that is removed from the sewage by the fine screen is MOST frequently   4.____

    A. blown by compressed air to the grit storage tank
    B. ground up and returned to the sewage
    C. burnt as fuel for the plant
    D. dried in the sludge drying beds and then disposed at sea

5. The one of the following pieces of equipment that is operated in conjunction with air pressure is a(n)   5.____

    A. centrifugal pump
    B. venturi
    C. ejector
    D. sump pump

6. One of the methods used to prime a centrifugal pump is to   6.____

    A. raise the air pressure in the pump
    B. bleed the suction line
    C. apply a vacuum to the pump
    D. open the suction valve

7. The one of the following types of pumps MOST frequently used to pump thickened sludge is the _____ type.   7.____

    A. ejector
    B. centrifugal
    C. gear
    D. piston

8. A plant is called an *Activated Sludge Plant* when the   8.____

    A. thickened sludge can be used as fertilizer
    B. gases from the sludge digestion tanks are burnt as fuel
    C. sludge must be dried before being disposed
    D. partly treated sewage is mixed with sludge

9. Where a digester tank has either a floating or a rising cover, it is made airtight by means of a(n)

    A. water seal
    B. sliding rubber gasket
    C. leather *bellows*
    D. oiled steel ring

10. Grease and fats are USUALLY removed from the sewage by

    A. skimming the liquid in the sedimentation tanks
    B. pumping the liquid from the sump in the grit chamber
    C. decanting the liquid in the digestion tank
    D. backwashing the fine screens

11. The type of plant in which *flocculation* MOST frequently occurs is the _____ plant.

    A. aerated sludge
    B. chemical precipitation
    C. plain screening
    D. filtration

12. Chlorine leaks are BEST detected by use of

    A. orthotoludin
    B. litmus paper
    C. ammonia
    D. copperas

13. Settling tanks operate effectively by _____ the sewage.

    A. slowing the speed of
    B. increasing the speed of
    C. changing the direction of flow of
    D. adding air to

14. A *venturi* is used in a sewage treatment plant in order to

    A. clean the diffusers
    B. control the amount of sewage in the wet well
    C. measure the flow of sewage
    D. reduce the pressure of the gases used as fuel

15. Sludge tanks are USUALLY heated by means of

    A. forced warm air
    B. hot water
    C. radiant heat
    D. electric coils

16. Chlorine is USUALLY added to sewage by

    A. adding the gas directly to the sewage
    B. mixing a small quantity of the sewage with the chlorine and then adding the mixture to the main body of sewage
    C. mixing the chlorine with water, and then adding the mixture to the sewage
    D. combining the gas with the air used in the aeration tank

17. The MAIN reason for defective operation of an aeration tank is that

    A. sewage flow is too slow
    B. of clogged diffuser plates
    C. tank temperature is too low
    D. too much air is supplied

18. The type of pump that seldom requires a relief valve is MOST likely a _____ pump.   18.____

    A. reciprocating   B. gear
    C. piston   D. centrifugal

19. The MAIN purpose of a foot valve in a centrifugal pump is to   19.____

    A. prevent the liquid from flowing back down the suction line
    B. equalize the pressure on both sides of the pump
    C. make it easier to prime the pump
    D. block passage of material that is too large to pump

20. The MAIN reason for lubricating machinery is to   20.____

    A. lower operating temperature
    B. keep down noise and vibration
    C. reduce friction
    D. lower cost of operation

21. The one of the following items that has the LOWEST viscosity is   21.____

    A. cup grease   B. kerosene
    C. #10 oil   D. #40 oil

22. The one of the following statements that is MOST NEARLY correct is: 22.____

    A. High speed machinery is most frequently lubricated by grease
    B. For most applications, either grease or oil can be used
    C. When in doubt, it is best to use the heavier of two grades of oil available
    D. Oil becomes *thinner* as the operating temperature increases

23. The function of a circuit breaker is MOST similar to that of a   23.____

    A. switch   B. fuse   C. rheostat   D. transformer

24. Noisy operation of a motor is MOST frequently caused by   24.____

    A. a shorted armature   B. over-voltage
    C. worn bearings   D. a grounded casing

25. Consumption of electrical energy is registered on a(n)   25.____

    A. volt-ohm meter   B. ammeter
    C. watt-hour meter   D. ohm meter

26. A dirty commutator is BEST cleaned by using   26.____

    A. sandpaper   B. soap and water
    C. emery cloth   D. kerosene

27. The one of the following items that is MOST frequently used to prevent an electric motor from being overloaded is a   27.____

    A. warning signal   B. governor
    C. thermal cut-out   D. rheostat

28. The one of the following metals that is MOST commonly used for outboard bearings is   28.____

    A. zinc   B. brass   C. magnesium   D. babbit

29. The use of pipe joint compound when making up a screwed joint results in a watertight joint and also

   A. cleans the threads
   B. makes the joint hard
   C. lubricates the threads
   D. prevents cross threading

30. A pipe is generally threaded by using a

   A. die   B. tap   C. yoke   D. swedge

31. The type of motor that MOST frequently does NOT use brushes is the

   A. universal type
   B. series wound D.C. motor
   C. synchronous motor
   D. induction motor

32. Compressed air can be used to clean generator and motor windings provided the air is

   A. heated
   B. blown at a high velocity
   C. used at a pressure of at least 90 lbs./sq.in.
   D. dry

33. The use of a cold chisel with a *mushroomed* head is

   A. *good*, because the mushrooming cushions the blow
   B. *bad*, because the head cannot be hit squarely
   C. *good*, because there is more area on the head to hit
   D. *bad*, because chips might fly from the head

34. After brass or black iron pipe has been cut, it should be

   A. counterbored
   B. reamed
   C. countersunk
   D. squared

35. The one of the following that is used to change the speed of certain types of electric motors is a (n)

   A. commutator
   B. brush
   C. rheostat
   D. armature

36. The type of pipe that is MOST frequently made with bell and spigot ends is

   A. brass
   B. steel
   C. cast iron
   D. transite

37. The one of the following that is used to connect two pipes together in a straight line is a

   A. manifold   B. divider   C. band   D. union

38. The difference between a stud and a bolt is that the stud has

   A. a finer thread
   B. no head
   C. a round head
   D. a coarser thread

39. A set screw is often used to

   A. bolt two pieces of flanged pipe together
   B. screw together matching parts in a motor casing
   C. clamp a piece to a work table
   D. secure a pulley to a shaft

40. Soft jaw inserts sometimes used to protect the surface of a piece of metal that is held in a vise are MOST frequently made of

   A. zinc   B. tin   C. brass   D. pewter

41. The BEST type of wrench to use on a large square nut is a _____ wrench.

   A. monkey   B. spanner   C. stillson   D. spintite

42. The BEST method of cleaning files is to use a

   A. file card   B. knife
   C. scriber   D. fibre brush

43. The BEST lubricant to use when cutting threads on steel pipe is _____ oil.

   A. pike   B. penetrating
   C. lard   D. coal

44. The BEST type of valve to use to control the flow of liquid to a delicate gauge is a _____ valve.

   A. gate   B. needle   C. globe   D. check

45. Water hammer is caused MAINLY by

   A. pumping sewage to too high a head
   B. interrupting the flow of sewage too rapidly
   C. debris floating in the sewage
   D. excessive corrosion in the pipes

46. Suppose a centrifugal pump is pumping less sewage than it is capable of handling. Of the following, the one that is NOT a possible reason for this is that the

   A. speed of pump is too slow
   B. pump is not properly primed
   C. stuffing box packing is defective
   D. suction line is partly clogged

47. The one of the following types of pumps that will give a smooth continuous flow of liquid rather than a pulsating flow is the _____ type.

   A. reciprocating   B. rotary
   C. gear   D. centrifugal

48. For pumping against a very high head, the BEST type of pump to use is a _____ type.

   A. reciprocating   B. propeller
   C. mixed flow   D. centrifugal

49. To increase the volume of delivery of a reciprocating pump, USUALLY the

    A. angle of the impeller is increased
    B. inlet valve is opened wider
    C. piston stroke is lengthened
    D. discharge valve is opened wider

50. The capacity of a pump is MOST frequently expressed in

    A. cubic feet per day
    B. gallons per day
    C. cubic feet per minute
    D. gallons per minute

KEY (CORRECT ANSWERS)

1. B	11. B	21. B	31. D	41. A
2. D	12. C	22. D	32. D	42. A
3. C	13. A	23. B	33. D	43. C
4. B	14. C	24. C	34. B	44. B
5. C	15. B	25. C	35. C	45. B
6. C	16. C	26. A	36. C	46. B
7. D	17. B	27. C	37. D	47. D
8. D	18. D	28. D	38. B	48. A
9. A	19. A	29. C	39. D	49. C
10. A	20. C	30. A	40. C	50. D

TEST 2

DIRECTIONS: Each question or incomplete statement is followed by several suggested answers or completions. Select the one that BEST answers the question or completes the statement. *PRINT THE LETTER OF THE CORRECT ANSWER IN THE SPACE AT THE RIGHT.*

1. The sum of the following dimensions: 1 5/8, 2 1/4, 4 1/16, 3 3/16, is 1.____
   A. 10 15/16   B. 11   C. 11 1/8   D. 11 1/4

2. Assume that six men, working together at the same rate of speed, can complete a certain job in 3 hours. 2.____
   If, however, there were only four men available to do this job, and they all worked at the same rate of speed, to complete this job would take MOST NEARLY _____ hours.
   A. 4 1/4   B. 4 1/2   C. 4 3/4   D. 5

3. Due to unforeseen difficulties, a job which would normally take 17 hours to complete was actually completed in 21 hours. 3.____
   This represents a percent increase over the normal time of MOST NEARLY
   A. 19%   B. 2.4%   C. 24%   D. 124%

4. The veteran should approach the problem of safety with the idea that 4.____
   A. there will always be accidents
   B. most accidents can be prevented
   C. the best method of preventing accidents is to post safety rules for the men to follow
   D. punishing the man with the worst accident record will reduce the number of accidents occurring

5. The one of the following that is NOT a common cause of accidents occurring when working around machinery is 5.____
   A. wearing loose clothing
   B. wearing gloves
   C. having insufficient illumination
   D. having slippery floors

Questions 6-8.

DIRECTIONS: Questions 6 through 8, inclusive, are to be answered in accordance with the following information.

A certain job requires 4 men working the number of hours and at the salary rate indicated in the accompanying table.

Name	No. of Hours	Salary/Hr.
Brown	30	$15.00
Jones	22	$19.50
Walter	40	$10.50
Thomas	25	$17.22

6. According to the above table, the salary received by Thomas on this job is MOST NEARLY

   A. $426.00 B. $427.50 C. $429.00 D. $430.50

7. According to the above table, the man who received the MOST wages chargeable to this job is

   A. Brown B. Jones C. Walter D. Thomas

8. According to the above table, the total amount of wages chargeable to this job is MOST NEARLY

   A. $1,726.50 B. $1,717.50 C. $1,729.50 D. $1,737.50

9. Of the following statements, the one that represents the SAFEST practice in a shop is: Adjustments should be made on.

   A. running machinery only if another man can be assigned to guard the man making the actual adjustment
   B. running machinery only if proper protective equipment is worn
   C. running machinery only when the machine is grounded
   D. machinery only after the machine has been stopped

10. Regarding work performed on electrical circuits, the one of the following that is unsafe is to

    A. use #10 wire instead of #12
    B. ground the junction boxes
    C. replace a 15 ampere circuit breaker with a 20 ampere one
    D. open the main switch before working on the wiring

11. Of the following, the MOST important reason for making detailed reports of all accidents is to

    A. have a record of who to blame for the accident
    B. be able to properly assess the cost of the accident
    C. reduce the number of *compensation* claims
    D. determine the causes of accidents and eliminate future accidents

12. As a veteran sewage treatment worker, you can BEST promote safety in your operations by

    A. carefully investigating and reporting the circumstances of any accident
    B. suggesting safer methods of operation
    C. training subordinates in proper safety
    D. disciplining subordinates who engage in unsafe acts

13. Oil-soaked rags are BEST stored in a

    A. neat pile in a readily accessible corner
    B. metal container with a tight cover
    C. metal box that has holes for adequate ventilation
    D. closet on a shelf above the ground

14. The one of the following actions that is NOT the cause of injury when working with hand tools is 14.____

    A. working with defective tools
    B. using the wrong tool for the job
    C. working too carefully
    D. using a tool improperly

15. Artificial respiration is the FIRST action you should take when a man becomes unconscious either as a result of drowning or as a result of 15.____

    A. chlorine poisoning   B. electric shock
    C. falling   D. clothing catching fire

Questions 16-17.

DIRECTIONS: Questions 16 and 17 should be answered in accordance with the following paragraph.

Sewage treatment plants are designed so that the sewage flow reaches the plant by gravity. In some instances, a small percentage of the sewerage system may be below the planned level of the plant. Economy in construction and other factors may indicate that the raising of that lower portion of the flow by means of pumps, to the desired plant elevation, is more desirable than lowering the plant structure. Some plants operate with this feature.

16. According to the above paragraph, 16.____

    A. a small percentage of the sewage reaches the plant by means of gravity
    B. all sewage reaches the plant by means of gravity
    C. where sewage cannot reach the plant by gravity it is pumped
    D. pumping is used so that all sewage can reach the plant

17. According to the above paragraph, the reason that some plants are built above the level of the sewerage system is that 17.____

    A. these plants operate more efficiently this way
    B. gravity will naturally bring the sewage in at a lower level
    C. pumping of the sewage is more expensive
    D. these plants are cheaper to build this way

Questions 18-20.

DIRECTIONS: Questions 18 through 20, inclusive, should be answered in accordance with the following paragraph.

Accident proneness is a subject which deserves much move objective and competent study than it has received to date. In discussing accident proneness, it is important to differentiate between the employee who is a "repeater" and one who is truly accident prone. It is obvious that any person put on work of which he knows little without thorough training in safe practice for the work in question will be liable to injury until he does learn the "how" of it. Few workmen left to their own devices will develop adequate safe practices. Therefore, they must be trained. Only those who fail to respond to proper training should be regarded as accident prone. The repeater whose accident record can be explained by a correctible physical defect, by correctible plant or machine hazards, by assignment to work for which he is not suited because of physical deficiencies or special abilities, cannot be fairly called "accident prone."

18. According to the above paragraph, a person is considered accident prone if

    A. he has accidents regardless of the fact that he has been properly trained
    B. he has many accidents
    C. it is possible for him to have accidents
    D. he works at a job where accidents are possible

19. According to the above paragraph,

    A. workers will learn the safe way of doing things if left to their own intelligence
    B. most workers must be trained to be safe
    C. a worker who has had more than one accident has not been properly trained
    D. intelligent workers are always safe

20. According to the above paragraph, a person would not be called accident prone if the cause of his accidents was

    A. a lack of interest in the job
    B. recklessness
    C. a low level of intelligence
    D. eyeglasses that don't fit properly

Questions 21-23.

DIRECTIONS: Questions 21 through 23, inclusive, should be answered in accordance with the following paragraph.

Sharpening a twist drill by hand is a skill that is mastered only after much practice and careful attention to the details. Therefore, whenever possible, use a tool grinder in which the drills can be properly positioned, clamped in place, and set with precision for the various angles. This machine grinding will enable you to sharpen the drills accurately. As a result, they will last longer and will produce more accurate holes.

21. According to the above paragraph, one reason for sharpening drills accurately is that the drills

    A. can then be used in a hand drill as well as a drill press
    B. will last longer
    C. can then be used by unskilled persons
    D. cost less

22. According to the above paragraph,

    A. it is easier to sharpen a drill by machine than by hand
    B. drills cannot be sharpened by hand
    C. only a skilled mechanic can learn to sharpen a drill by hand
    D. a good mechanic will learn to sharpen drills by hand

23. As used in the above paragraph, the word *precision* means MOST NEARLY

    A. accuracy   B. ease   C. rigidity   D. speed

Questions 24-27.

DIRECTIONS: Questions 24 through 27, inclusive, should be answered in accordance with the following paragraph.

Centrifugal pumps have relatively fewer moving parts than reciprocating pumps, and no valves. While reciprocating pumps when new are usually more efficient than centrifugal pumps, the latter retain their efficiency longer. Most rotary pumps are also without valves, but they have closely meshed parts between which high pressures may be set up after they begin to wear. In general, centrifugal pumps can be made much smaller than reciprocating pumps giving the same result. There is an exception, in that positive displacement pumps delivering small volumes at high heads are smaller than equivalent centrifugal pumps. Centrifugal pumps cost less when first purchased than other comparable pumps. The original outlay may be as little as one-third or one-half that of a reciprocating pump suitable for the same purpose.

24. The type of pump NOT mentioned in the above paragraph is the _____ type. 24._____

    A. rotary
    B. propeller
    C. reciprocating
    D. centrifugal

25. According to the above paragraph, the type of pump that sometimes has valves and sometimes does NOT is the 25._____

    A. rotary
    B. propeller
    C. reciprocating
    D. centrifugal

26. According to the above paragraph, centrifugal pumps are 26._____

    A. *always smaller* than reciprocating pumps
    B. *smaller* than reciprocating pumps only when designed to deliver small quantities at low pressures
    C. *larger* than reciprocating pumps only when designed to deliver small quantities at high pressures
    D. *larger* than reciprocating pumps only when designed to deliver large quantities at low pressures

27. The advantage of centrifugal pumps that is NOT mentioned in the above paragraph is that 27._____

    A. the centrifugal pump retains its efficiency longer
    B. it is impossible to create an excessive pressure when using a centrifugal pump
    C. there are fewer parts to wear out in a centifugal pump
    D. the centrifugal pump is cheaper

Questions 28-30.

DIRECTIONS: Questions 28 through 30, inclusive, should be answered in accordance with the following paragraph.

Gaskets made of relatively soft materials are placed between the meeting surfaces of hydraulic fittings in order to increase the tightness of the seal. They should be composed of materials that will not be affected by the liquid to be enclosed, nor by the conditions under which the system operates, including maximum pressure and temperature. They should be able to maintain the amount of clearance required between meeting surfaces. One of the materials most widely used in making gaskets is neoprene. Since neoprene is flexible, it is often used in sheet form at points where a gasket must expand enough to allow air to accumulate, as with cover plates on supply tanks. Over a period of time, oil tends to deteriorate the material used in making neoprene gaskets. The condition of the gasket must, therefore, be checked whenever the unit is disassembled. Since neoprene gasket material is soft and flexible, it easily becomes misshapen, scratched or torn. Great care is, therefore, necessary in handling neoprene. Shellac, gasket sealing compounds or "pipe dope" should never be used with sheet neoprene, unless absolutely necessary for satisfactory installation.

28. Of the following, the one that is NOT mentioned in the above paragraph as a requirement for a good gasket material is that the material must be

    A. cheap
    B. unaffected by heat developed in a system
    C. relatively soft
    D. capable of maintaining required clearances

29. According to the above paragraph, neoprene will be affected by

    A. air
    B. temperature
    C. pressure
    D. oil

30. According to the above paragraph, care is necessary in handling neoprene because

    A. its condition must be checked frequently
    B. it tears easily
    C. pipe dope should not be used
    D. it is difficult to use

Questions 31-35.

DIRECTIONS: Questions 31 through 35, inclusive, should be answered in accordance with the following statements and instructions.

Column A below lists defects that often happen to equipment that is used in a sewage disposal plant. Column B shows the equipment that is used in such a plant. In the space at the right next to the number of the defect listed in Column A, select the letter in Column B representing the piece of equipment with which this defect is MOST closely associated.

COLUMN A	COLUMN B
31. Broken shear pin	A. Centrifugal pump
32. Worn collector ring	B. Wound rotor motor
33. Pitted impeller	C. Bar screen
34. Worn chain	D. Methane-gas engine
35. Crankpin bearing	

36. It is often said that in selecting a man for a job, dependability is more important than seniority. This is because 36._____

    A. it is difficult to judge the amount of work an older man can do
    B. an older man will know how to *avoid* work better
    C. the dependable man is the man you can count on to do the job as called for
    D. the dependable man will require fewer instructions

37. *A man may be conscientious, and yet not be efficient.* This statement MOST likely means that 37._____

    A. a man will not be able to do a job properly unless he has special training
    B. a man may want to do a job well, but may not know how to go about doing it
    C. if a man is efficient, he may not be conscientious
    D. the more conscientious a man is the less efficient he will be

38. If you were a senior sewage treatment worker, a good way of building up the morale of men assigned to you would be to 38._____

    A. overlook minor infractions of the rules
    B. pass the blame for bad assignments to your superiors
    C. treat the men fairly
    D. cover up for men who have made mistakes in their jobs

39. Threatening your subordinates with penalties for neglect of duty is 39._____

    A. *good* practice just to frighten them, even though the penalties will not be inflicted
    B. *poor* practice since men should never be threatened
    C. *good* practice if the penalty is actually going to be inflicted
    D. *poor* practice because men ought to work properly without threats

40. Of the following, the BEST indication that men are dissatisfied with their jobs is that they 40._____

    A. offer suggestions on improving operations
    B. appoint a grievance committee
    C. all join a union
    D. frequently leave for other jobs

41. If a senior sewage treatment worker must reprimand one of the men under him, the reprimand should be given 41._____

    A. in a loud tone of voice so that the man is properly impressed
    B. firmly but quietly
    C. the next day when the senior can get the man alone
    D. in front of the entire crew so that the rest of the men know what is right

42. If a senior sewage treatment worker is not sure of how a job should be done, he should 42._____

    A. make believe he does so that his men will not discover his lack of knowledge
    B. get someone else to do the job
    C. ask his superior how the job should be done
    D. put the job off until he can learn from another crew how it should be done

43. A senior sewage treatment worker makes a mistake, and admits it to his men. This practice is _____, because the men _____.

   A. *good;* will respect him more
   B. *poor;* will not trust his judgment anymore
   C. *good;* will then learn to check everything he does before wasting time doing jobs improperly
   D. *poor;* should not know why a job is being done in the way it is

44. A supervisor can BEST earn the respect of his men by

   A. never criticizing his men
   B. taking the blame for all actions of his men
   C. defending his men from all criticism, regardless of whether the criticism is deserved or not
   D. defending his men from unsupported criticism

45. As a senior sewage treatment worker, you have been ordered by the engineer to do a job in a certain manner which you think is not a good way of doing the job. You should

   A. tell the engineer you should be permitted to do the job in whatever way you feel best
   B. avoid doing the job
   C. do the job, but tell your men that you are not responsible for the method being used
   D. explain your objections to the engineer, but then do the job in whatever manner the engineer decides

46. The MOST important requirement for a good supervisor is to have

   A. physical strength   B. the ability to handle men
   C. manual dexterity   D. good appearance

47. A good senior sewage treatment worker should

   A. give all the disagreeable assignments to the laziest worker
   B. give all the good assignments to the best worker
   C. give disagreeable assignments to those men who have special training for them
   D. rotate disagreeable assignments among the men

48. A new sewage treatment worker has been assigned to work under you as a senior. The MOST important information you should get from the new man is

   A. his age
   B. the type of work he likes to do
   C. his previous experience
   D. how well he gets along with other men

49. A member of your crew, who frequently comes to you with unjustified complaints, comes to you again with another complaint.
You should

   A. cut the man short and tell him to stop complaining unnecessarily
   B. listen to the complaint, but do nothing about it
   C. listen to the complaint, and then tell the man the complaint is not justified
   D. check the complaint to see if it is justified

50. To insure that the men working under him are doing their work properly, a senior sewage treatment worker should

    A. check their work frequently
    B. have the men prepare a written report about the work
    C. assign one individual to be responsible for each job
    D. keep a record of the supplies they use

KEY (CORRECT ANSWERS)

1. C	11. D	21. B	31. C	41. B
2. B	12. C	22. A	32. B	42. C
3. C	13. B	23. A	33. A	43. A
4. B	14. C	24. B	34. C	44. D
5. B	15. B	25. A	35. D	45. D
6. D	16. B	26. C	36. C	46. B
7. A	17. D	27. B	37. B	47. D
8. C	18. A	28. A	38. C	48. C
9. D	19. B	29. D	39. C	49. D
10. C	20. D	30. B	40. D	50. A

EXAMINATION SECTION
TEST 1

DIRECTIONS: Each question or incomplete statement is followed by several suggested answers or completions. Select the one that BEST answers the question or completes the statement. PRINT THE LETTER OF THE CORRECT ANSWER IN THE SPACE AT THE RIGHT.

1. In a modification of the conventional activated sludge process known as Modified Aeration, the percentage of returned sludge to the aeration tank is, MOST nearly,

    A. 10   B. 20   C. 30   D. 40

2. The amount of chlorine, in pounds per million gallons, to produce 0.5 ppm residual in most primary effluents will, *most nearly*, be between

    A. 10 to 40   B. 50 to 70   C. 100 to 200   D. 300 to 500

3. In a conventional activated sludge treatment plant, air is applied at a rate of, most *nearly*,

    A. 1 to 1 1/2 cubic feet per gallon of sewage
    B. 3 to 3 1/2 cubic feet per gallon of sewage
    C. 4 to 5 1/2 cubic feet per gallon of sewage
    D. 7 to 7 1/2 cubic feet per gallon of sewage

4. Of the following temperature ranges, the *one* which is the MOST efficient for sludge digester operation is

    A. 45° F and 50° F   B. 55° F and 65° F
    C. 70° F and 75° F   D. 85° F and 95° F

5. The sewage detention time in an aeration tank using modified aeration is, *most nearly*,

    A. 2 hours   B. 4 hours   C. 6 hours   D. 8 hours

6. The BTU per cubic foot value of sludge gas from a well established and properly operated digestion tank is, most *nearly*,

    A. 150   B. 350   C. 450   D. 650

7. BOD is an abbreviation for

    A. Bacteria Operating Demand
    B. Biosorption Operating Demand
    C. Biochemical Oxygen Demand
    D. Biofilter Oxygen Demand

8. The one of the following that is normally used to control the flow of sewage to the treatment plant from the intercepting sewer is the

    A. float valve   B. sluice gate
    C. gate valve   D. regulator gate

9. A sludge gas encountered at sewage treatment plants that is corrosive and damaging to metals is

   A. carbon dioxide
   B. ethane
   C. nitrogen
   D. hydrogen sulphide

10. When sludge is withdrawn from a sludge gas collector tank with a fixed color, a compensating volume of fresh sludge or water or gas must be put into the tank to prevent the development of

    A. leakage
    B. positive pressures
    C. negative pressures
    D. condensation

11. Devices in sewage treatment plants whose function is to break or cut up solids found in sewage are known as

    A. barmimutors
    B. diffusers
    C. tricklers
    D. grinders

12. The sludge treatment process whereby the volume of sludge going to the digester is reduced is known as

    A. thickening
    B. elutriation
    C. chemical conditioning
    D. wet oxidation

13. *Most* of the suspended solids are separated or removed from the sewage by

    A. aeration   B. washing   C. elutriation   D. sedimentation

14. The *one* of the following that is usually operated by compressed air is a

    A. reducer
    B. baffle
    C. sump pump
    D. sewage ejector

15. The PRIMARY function of a grit chamber in a sewage treatment plant is to remove

    A. paper   B. worms   C. gravel   D. algae

16. A deep two-storied storage sewage tank with an upper sedimentaton chamber and a lower chamber is known as a _____ tank.

    A. detritus   B. imhoff   C. septic   D. elocculating

17. The *one* of the following which BEST characterizes activated sludge is that it is

    A. black in color and has small particles
    B. blue in color and has large particles
    C. brown in color and has some dissolved oxygen
    D. beige in color and has a great amount of dissolved oxygen

18. The *optimum* PH value of the sludge in a digester should be

    A. 10   B. 7   C. 3   D. 2

19. In the Activated Sludge Process, the *one* of the following steps that may be taken to prevent or control sludge bulkings is to

    A. decrease aeration in time and rate
    B. chlorinate returned activated sludge

C. increase the solids content carried in aeration tanks
D. raise the pH value to 7.8

20. In starting a digester unit, the QUICKEST results can be obtained by

    A. seeding   B. shredding   C. dosing   D. chlorinating

21. Sludge digestion carried out in the absence of free oxygen is known as

    A. wet oxidation   B. heat drying
    C. anaerobic decomposition   D. aerobic decomposition

22. "Frothing" is MOST frequently attributable to

    A. short circuiting of aeration tanks
    B. septic sewage in primary tank
    C. high concentration of fungus
    D. detergent compounds in the sewage

23. The process of removing floating grease or scum from the surface of sewage in a tank is called

    A. squeegeeing   B. siphoning
    C. skimming   D. sloughing

24. Of the following, the one which BEST represents a primary treatment device for sewage is the

    A. stabilization pond   B. intermittent sand filter
    C. septic tank   D. aeration tank

25. Freshly poured concrete surfaces normally exposed to air should be cured for a minimum period of

    A. 4 days   B. 5 days   C. 6 days   D. 7 days

26. One of your men on the job is injured at a work site and is unconscious. The BEST course of action for you to follow is to

    A. give him liquids to drink
    B. have him remain in a lying position until medical help arrives
    C. immediately move him to the first-aid station
    D. attempt to arouse him to consciousness by shaking him

27. The type of portable fire extinguisher that is MOST effective in controlling a fire around live electrical equipment is the

    A. foam type   B. soda-acid type
    C. carbon-dioxide type   D. water type

28. The hazards of electric shock resulting from operation of a portable electric tool in a damp location can be reduced by

    A. grounding the tool
    B. holding the tool with one hand
    C. running the tool at low speed
    D. using a baffle

4 (#1)

29. The *one* of the following that is the *proper* first aid to administer to a conscious person suffering from chlorine inhalation is

    A. an alocholic drink
    B. black coffee
    C. a pulmotor
    D. a cold shower

29.___

30. Of the following actions, the *best one* to take FIRST after smoke is seen coming from an electric control device is to

    A. shut off the power to it
    B. call the main office for advice
    C. look for a wiring diagram
    D. throw water on it

30.___

KEY (CORRECT ANSWERS)

1.	A	16.	B
2.	C	17.	C
3.	A	18.	B
4.	D	19.	B
5.	A	20.	A
6.	D	21.	C
7.	C	22.	D
8.	B	23.	C
9.	D	24.	C
10.	C	25.	D
11.	A	26.	B
12.	A	27.	C
13.	D	28.	A
14.	D	29.	B
15.	C	30.	A

TEST 2

DIRECTIONS: Each question or incomplete statement is followed by several suggested answers or completions. Select the one that *BEST* answers the question or completes the statement. *PRINT THE LETTER OF THE CORRECT ANSWER IN THE SPACE AT THE RIGHT.*

1. Of the following, the *BEST* fastener to use when attaching a pipe support bracket to a concrete wall is a(n) 1.____

   A. toggle bolt
   B. expansion bolt
   C. carriage bolt
   D. lag bolt

2. The *MAIN* reason for mixing a "thinner" into paint is to 2.____

   A. *clear up* air bubbles
   B. *stop* the paint from bleeding
   C. *spread* the paint easily
   D. *make* the paint color lighter

3. Schedule 40 pipe is a designation for 3.____

   A. asbestos cement pipe
   B. steel pipe
   C. transite pipe
   D. clay pipe

4. The function of a check valve in a pipeline is to 4.____

   A. relieve excessive pressure
   B. remove air
   C. meter the flow
   D. prevent reverse flow

5. The device on an electric motor which will prevent overheating is called a 5.____

   A. rheostat
   B. bus bar
   C. solenoid
   D. thermal relay

6. The oil recommended for the gear box of a 20-ton sewage plant crane is, *most nearly,* 6.____

   A. SAE 80   B. SAE 120   C. SAE 160   D. SAE 200

7. Where pump ball bearings may be subjected to water washing, the lubricating grease should have a 7.____

   A. white lead base
   B. red lead base
   C. sodium soap base
   D. lithum soap base

8. A chlorine leak can normally be detected by 8.____

   A. a lighted candle
   B. its smell
   C. a dry rag
   D. an oil-soaked rag

9. The moving wooden planks in a tank used to scrape sludge from the bottom of a tank are known as 9.____

   A. cleats   B. flights   C. rails   D. levers

10. A device with an edge or notch used for measuring liquid flow is known as a 10.____

    A. Parshall Flume
    B. Plainer Bowlus
    C. Venturi
    D. Weir

11. The *one* of the following types of pumps that is WIDELY used for pumping sewage is

    A. reciprocating B. rotary C. simplex D. centrifugal

12. Prior to starting a newly installed pump, you should

    A. open the motor disconnect switch
    B. expose the pump to outside weather conditions
    C. turn the shaft by hand to see that it rotates freely
    D. disconnect the vent and drain the plugs

13. A maintenance program for a new piece of operating equipment should BEST be set up in accordance with the

    A. location of the unit
    B. location of personnel
    C. manufacturer's recommendations
    D. monthly plant capacity

14. The *one* of the following fasteners that has threads at *both* ends is called a

    A. screw B. stud C. blivet D. drift bolt

15. The *one* of the following that is installed between two pipe flanges to seal the connection is called a

    A. sheave B. gasket C. boss D. fillet

16. A wet undigested sludge containing a large amount of grease will MOST probably

    A. clog the opening of the filter
    B. have no effect on the efficiency of the filters
    C. cause rapid deterioration of the filter
    D. cause the filter to shrink and snap

17. The floating cover for a sludge gas storage tank is kept under a gauge pressure of, *most nearly,*

    A. 0 to 2 ounces   B. 3 to 5 ounces
    C. 6 to 9 ounces   D. 10 to 12 ounces

18. The tool that is used to remove the burrs from the end of 1/2" diameter steel pipe after cutting it with a pipe cutter is known as a

    A. bit B. reamer C. tap D. caliper

19. Of the following common obstructions found in sewer lines, the *one* that occurs MOST frequently is

    A. roots B. debris C. grease D. grit

20. The *one* of the following that is the MAIN reason for putting orders in writing is to

    A. protect the person who receives it
    B. protect the person who prepared the order
    C. make it easier to check mistakes
    D. protect the agency should something unforeseen occur

21. For records to provide an essential basis for future changes or expansions of the sewage treatment plant, the records must be

    A. accurate
    B. lengthy
    C. detailed in ink
    D. hand-written in pencil

22. The volume, in cubic feet, of a slab of concrete that is 5'-0" wide, 6'-0" long, and 0'-6" in depth is, *most nearly,*

    A. 15.0   B. 13.5   C. 12.0   D. 10.5

23. The sum of the following pipe lengths, 22 1/8", 7 3/4", 19 7/16", and 4 3 5/8", is:

    A. 91 7/8"   B. 92 1/16"   C. 92 1/4"   D. 92 15/16"

24. The area in square feet of a plant floor that is 42 feet wide and 75 feet long is

    A. 3150   B. 3100   C. 3075   D. 2760

25. Of the following types of gauges, the *one* that indicates pressure above and below atmospheric pressures is known as a

    A. pressure   B. vacuum   C. Bourdan   D. compound

26. A U-tube manometer is used to measure

    A. deflection   B. height   C. radiation   D. pressure

27. If an air-conditioning unit shorted out and caught fire, the BEST fire extinguisher to use would be a _____ extinguisher.

    A. water
    B. foam
    C. carbon dioxide
    D. soda acid

28. Of the following, the *best* action to take to help someone whose eyes have been splashed with lye is to FIRST

    A. wash out the eyes with clean water
    B. wash out the eyes with a salt water solution
    C. apply a sterile dressing over the eyes
    D. do nothing to the eyes, but telephone for medical help

Questions 29-30.

DIRECTIONS: Questions numbered 29 and 30 are to be answered in accordance with the information given in the following paragraph:

A sludge lagoon is an excavated area in which digested sludge is desired. Lagoon depths vary from six to eight feet. There are no established criteria for the required capacity of a lagoon. The sludge moisture content is reduced by evaporation and drainage. Volume reduction is slow, especially in cold and rainy weather. Weather and soil conditions affect concentration. The drying period ranges from a period of several months to several years. After the sludge drying period has ended, a bulldozer or tractor can be used to remove the sludge. The dried sludge can be used for fill of low ground. A filled dried lagoon can be developed into a lawn. Lagoons can be used for emergency storage when the sludge beds are full. Lagoons are popular because they are inexpensive to build and operate. They have a disadvantage of being unsightly. A hazard to lagoon operation is the possibility of draining partly digested sludge to the lagoon that creates a fly and odor nuisance.

29. In accordance with the given paragraph, sludge lagoons have the *disadvantage* of being   29._____

    A. unsightly
    B. too deep
    C. concentrated
    D. wet

30. In accordance with the given paragraph, moisture content is *reduced* by   30._____

    A. digestion
    B. evaporation
    C. oxidation
    D. removal

KEY (CORRECT ANSWERS)

1.	B	16.	A
2.	C	17.	B
3.	B	18.	B
4.	D	19.	A
5.	D	20.	B
6.	B	21.	A
7.	D	22.	A
8.	B	23.	D
9.	B	24.	A
10.	D	25.	D
11.	D	26.	D
12.	C	27.	C
13.	C	28.	A
14.	B	29.	A
15.	A	30.	B

BASIC FUNDAMENTALS OF SEWAGE TREATMENT AND DISPOSAL

CONTENTS

	Page
CHAPTER 1: SEWAGE	1
Sources of Sewage and Wastes	1
Definitions	2
Appearance of Sewage	3
Composition of Sewage	3
Solids in Sewage	3
Definitions of Solids in Sewage	4
Dissolved Gases	5
Biological Composition Sewage	5
Condition of Sewage	8
Chemical Changes in Sewage Composition	8
CHAPTER 2: SEWAGE DISPOSAL	12
Sewage Treatment	12
Sewage Disposal	12
Role of Dissolved Oxygen in Receiving Waters	13
Biochemical Oxygen Demand (BOD)	13
Self-purification	14
Need for Sewage Treatment	15
Legal Aspects of Sewage Disposal	17
CHAPTER 3: SEWAGE TREATMENT METHODS	19
Preliminary Treatment	19
Primary Treatment	20
Secondary Treatment	20
Chlorination	21
Sludge Treatment	21
Package Units	21
CHAPTER 4: PRELIMINARY TREATMENT	22
Racks and Bar Screens	22
Fine Screens	22
Comminuting Devices	22
Grit Chambers	23
Pre-aeration Tanks	24
CHAPTER 5: PRIMARY TREATMENT	25
Septic Tanks	25
Two-story Tanks	26
Plain Sedimentation Tanks	30
Chemical Treatment	34

CHAPTER 6: SECONDARY TREATMENT 37
   Trickling Filters 37
   Second Sedimentation Tanks.. 45
   Activated Sludge 45
   Modifications of the Conventional Activated Sludge Process.................................. 50
   Operation of Activated Sludge Process 52
   Contact Aeration 54
   Intermittent Sand Filters 55
   Stabilization Ponds.. 56

CHAPTER 1

SEWAGE

Sewage is largely the water supply of a community after it has been fouled by various uses. From the standpoint of source, it may be a combination of the liquid or water-carried wastes from residences, business buildings, and institutions, together with those from industrial establishments, and with such ground water, surface and storm water as may be present.

Volume. The amount or volume of sewage produced varies in different communities depending on a number of factors. A strictly residential community with well-constructed sewers from which storm waters are excluded might average 40 gallons per person per day while an industrial community or one in which the domestic use of water is unusually high may have 200 gallons or more per person per day requiring disposal. In the United States, a figure of 100 gallons per person per day has been considered a reasonable average, though this figure is tending to increase with the growing use of automatic laundry and dishwashing machines and garbage grinders. Where storm waters are admitted to the sewers carrying domestic and industrial wastes, the average is, of course, much higher.

SOURCES OF SEWAGE AND WASTES

Sewage originates from several different sources:
1. Human and animal wastes
2. Household wastes
3. Storm flows
4. Ground water infiltration
5. Industrial wastes

1. *Human and Animal Wastes*: These consist of the body discharges which become part of sewage through flushing of toilet facilities, and to some extent those of animals which are washed into sewers from soil or streets. These wastes are the most important as affecting public health because they may contain organisms which produce disease in man and their safe and effective treatment constitutes a major problem in conditioning sewage for disposal.

2. *Household Wastes*: These are derived from home laundry operations, bathing, kitchen wastes, from washing and cooking foods and dishwashing. Most of these contain soaps, synthetic detergents usually containing foaming agents now generally used in housekeeping. Kitchen wastes have particles of food and greases which are becoming a more significant and increasing part of household wastes with the growing use of home garbage grinding units.

3. *Street Washings and Storm Flows*: Rains and storms deposit varying amounts of water on the land, much of which drains or washes over the surface and carries with it grit, sand, leaves, and other debris that may be lying on the drained surfaces. In some communities, this storm drainage is allowed to flow into the sewers or collecting devices for the community wastes and becomes an important component of the sewage. In other communities, these flows are collected separately for disposal and do not become a part

1

of the community sewage. Storm flow volume varies with the intensity of rainfall, topography, and pavements and roof areas. Storm waters from roof areas are of particular significance with respect to the volume of sewage to be treated when they are connected, usually illegally, to sewers from which they are supposedly excluded.

4. *Ground Water Infiltration*: Sewers, the collecting devices for sewage, are buried in the ground and in many instances are laid below ground water levels, particularly when such levels are high because of excessive seasonal rainfall. Since the joints between sections of the pipe forming the sewers are not all tight, an opportunity exists for the flow of ground water, or infiltration, into the sewers. Collecting sewers are usually not under pressure, the flow in them being by gravity only, and consequently such infiltration is not only possible but at times is considerable. The volume of ground water infiltration cannot be determined accurately. It is influenced by soil composition, the type of sewer construction, ground water conditions, and rainfall and other weather conditions.

5. *Industrial Wastes*: The waste products of manufacturing processes are an important part of community sewage and their effective disposal must be provided for. In many areas industrial or manufacturing wastes are collected with other community components of sewage for ultimate treatment and disposal. These wastes vary widely in type and volume, depending on the manufacturing establishments located in the community. In some instances the volume and character of industrial wastes are such that separate collecting and disposal devices must be provided. Many types of industrial wastes contain frothing or foaming agents, detergents, and other chemical substances that interfere with the final disposal of the community sewage or damage sewers and other structures. Thus, they cannot be added directly to the sewage but must be given a preliminary treatment or disposed of by separate and special means.

DEFINITIONS

Descriptive names have been given to the various types of sewage depending on their sources as described above. These are defined as follows:

Domestic sewage is that containing human and animal wastes and household wastes. Ground water infiltration is also included. This sewage is typical of residential areas where there are no or only very minor industrial operations.

Sanitary sewage is commonly considered to be the same as domestic sewage. It includes all of the domestic sewage but may also contain much, if not all, of the industrial wastes of the community.

Storm waters consist of the surface run off from storms, flowing from roofs, pavements, and over natural ground surfaces.

Combined sewage is a mixture of domestic or sanitary sewage and storm waters when both are collected in the same sewers.

Industrial wastes are the waste waters from manufacturing processes. They may be collected and disposed of by themselves or may be added to and become part of sanitary or combined sewage.

APPEARANCE OF SEWAGE

Sewage is a turbid liquid containing solid material in suspension. When fresh it is gray in color, and has a musty and not unpleasant odor. It carries varying amounts and kinds of floating matter; fecal solids, bits of food, garbage, paper, sticks, and other types of material disposed of in the daily life of a community of people. With the passage of time, the color gradually changes from gray to black, foul and unpleasant odors develop and black solids appear floating on the surface or throughout the liquid. In this state, it is termed septic sewage.

COMPOSITION OF SEWAGE

Sewage consists of water plus solids which are dissolved or carried in suspension in the water. The solids are very small in amount, usually less than 0.1 percent by weight, but they are the part of the sewage that presents the major problems in its adequate treatment and disposal. The water provides only the volume and a vehicle for transportation of the solids.

These solids may be dissolved, suspending, or floating. Advertising slogans for a certain brand of soap has established as an acceptable standard the idea of 99.44 percent pure. An average domestic sewage, consisting of over 99.44 percent water meets an even stricter standard of purity. However, the less than 0.1 percent solids portion of sewage is a much more potent and significantly impurity than the 0.56 percent impurity of the soap product.

SOLIDS IN SEWAGE

The solids in sewage may be divided into two general groups, depending on their composition or on their physical condition. Thus, we have the organic and inorganic solids which may in turn be suspended and dissolved solids. These groupings are shown in Figure 1 with definitions following the figure.

FIGURE 1
PHYSICAL CONDITION AND COMPOSITION OF SOLIDS
IN AN AVERAGE DOMESTIC SEWAGE
(Numbers are in parts per million)

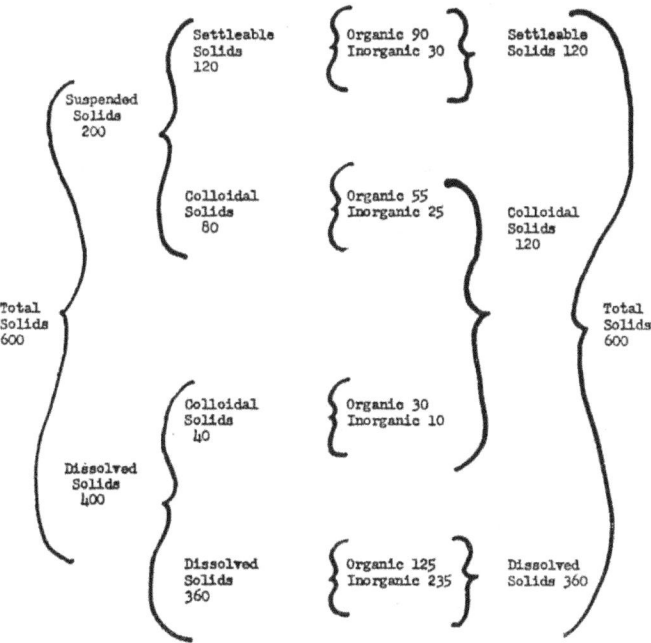

3

DEFINITIONS OF SOLIDS IN SEWAGE

Organic Solids: These are generally of animal or vegetable origin including the waste products of animal and vegetable life, dead animal matter, plant tissue, or organisms, but may include synthetic organic compounds. They are substances which contain carbon, hydrogen, and oxygen, some of which may be combined with nitrogen, sulphur or phosphorus. The principal groups are proteins, carbohydrates, and fats, together with the products of their decomposition. They are subject to decay or decomposition through the activity of bacteria and other living organisms and are combustible, that is, they can be burned.

Inorganic solids are those substances which are inert and not subject to decay. Exceptions to this characteristic are certain mineral compounds or salts—such as sulfates—which under certain conditions, to be discussed in detail later, can be broken down to simpler substances such as the reduction of sulfates to sulfides. Inorganic solids are frequently designate as mineral substances and include sand, gravel, silt, and the mineral salts in the water supply which produce the hardness and mineral content of the water. In general, they are noncombustible.

The amount of these solids, both organic and inorganic, in sewage, imparts to it what is frequently termed its *strength*. Actually, the amount of concentration of the organic solids and their capacity to undergo decay or decomposition is the principal part of this strength. The greater the concentration of organic solids, the stronger the sewage. A *strong sewage* can be defined as one containing a large amount of solids, particularly organic solids. A *weak sewage* is one containing only a small amount of organic solids.

As already noted, solids can be grouped depending on their physical state as suspended solids, colloidal solids, and dissolved solids, each of which may include both organic and inorganic solids.

Suspended solids are those which are visible and in suspension in the water. They are the solids which can be removed from the sewage by physical or mechanical means, such as sedimentation or filtration. More exactly, they are the solids which are retained on the asbestos mat filter in a Gooch crucible. They include the larger floating particles and consist of sand, grit, clay, fecal solids, paper, sticks of wood, particles of food and garbage, and similar materials. They are about 70 percent organic solids and 30 percent inorganic solids, the latter being principally sand and grit.

Suspended solids are divided into two parts—settleable solids and colloidal solids.

Settleable solids are that portion of the suspended solids which are of sufficient size and weight to settle in a given period of time, usually one hour. As used in this Manual, they are those which will settle in an Imhoff cone in one hour. They are usually reported as millimeters of solids per liter of sewage, but may be reported as parts per million by weight gas given in Figure 1. They are about 75 percent organic and 25 percent inorganic.

Colloidal Suspended Solids: These are somewhat loosely defined as the difference between the total suspended solids and the settleable solids. There is, at present, no simple or standard laboratory tests to specifically determine colloidal matter. Some will settle out if the quiescent period in the Imhoff cone test is longer than one hour, but most will remain in suspension over long periods of several days or more. They constitute that portion of the total suspended solids (about 40 percent) which are not readily removed by physical or mechanical treatment facilities but will not pass the asbestos mat filter in a Gooch crucible. In composition they are about two-thirds organic and one-third inorganic, are subject to rapid decay, and are an important factor in the treatment and disposal of sewage.

Dissolved Solids: The term "dissolved solids as commonly used in discussing sewage is not technically correct. All of these solids are not in true solution but they include some solids in the colloidal state. As used, the term means all of the solids which pass through the asbestos filter in a Gooch crucible. Of the total dissolved solids, about 90 percent are in true solution and about ten percent colloidal. Dissolved solids, as a whole, are about 40 percent organic and 60 percent inorganic. The colloidal portion is higher in percent organic matter than the solids in true solution as the latter includes all of the mineral salts in the water supply.

Total Solids, as the term implies, includes all of the solid constituents of sewage. They are the total of the organic and inorganic solids or the total of the suspended and dissolved solids. In an average domestic sewage, they are about half organic and half inorganic, and about two-thirds in solution and one-third in suspension. It is the organic half of the solids, which are subject to decay, that constitute the main problem in sewage treatment.

As already noted, the weights of the various types of solids as given in Figure 1, and as carried through the definitions, are based on an average domestic sewage, equivalent to approximately 100 gallons per capita per day. Addition of storm water flows or ground water infiltration may change those solids relationships markedly. Similarly, the introduction of industrial wastes may increase the solids content, particularly the organic solids, with very definite variations in the strength of the sewage. Also, sewage varies widely in both composition and volume from hour to hour, depending upon changes in community activities. Obviously, sewage is likely to be at its maximum strength and flow during the daytime and be at a minimum during the night hours. Also, sewage may vary in its composition from day to day with corresponding changes in the industrial and community activities from which the sewage originates. On Sundays and weekends and holidays, flows and strengths are frequently reduced because of the lowered rate of communal activity. Any table of sewage composition can give only an average composition. The amounts of solids indicated cannot be applied equally to all sewages at all times.

DISSOLVED GASES

Sewage contains small and varying concentrations of dissolved gases. Among the most important of these is oxygen, present in the original water supply and also dissolved from air in contact with the surface of flowing sewage. This oxygen, familiarly known as *dissolved oxygen*, is an exceedingly important component of sewage and its functions will be discussed in detail below. In addition to dissolved oxygen, sewage may contain other gases, such as *carbon dioxide*, resulting from the decomposition of organic matter; *nitrogen* dissolved from the atmosphere; *hydrogen sulfide* formed by the decomposition of organic and certain inorganic sulfur compounds. These gases, although small in amount, function importantly in the decomposition and treatment of sewage solids and signify to a major degree the progress of such treatment procedures.

Volatile Liquids. Sewage may contain volatile liquids. These are, in general, liquids which boil at less than 212 degrees Fahrenheit, as, for example, gasoline.

BIOLOGICAL COMPOSITION OF SEWAGE

Sewage also contains countless numbers of living organisms, most of them too small in size to be visible except when viewed under a microscope. They are a natural living part of the organic matter found in sewage and their presence is of utmost importance because they are one of the reasons for sewage treatment and the success of such treatment, involving decay or decomposition, is dependent upon their activities. It can well be said that they are the workers used by a sewage treatment plant operator and his success may be measured by his knowledge of and attention to their likes and dislikes in their eating habits and environment.

These microscopic living organisms may be considered to be of two general types: bacteria and other more complex living organisms.

Bacteria: Bacteria are living organisms, microscopic in size, which consist of a single cell and are similar in functions and life processes to plants. Some bacteria are *motile*, able to move about freely by their own power, and others are *non-motile*. Like all living organisms, bacteria require food, oxygen and water. They can exist only when the environment provides these necessities. In turn, they produce waste products as the result of their life processes.

Bacteria can be divided into two main groups: Parasitic bacteria and Saprophytic bacteria.

Parasitic bacteria are those which normally live off of another living organism, known as the host, since they require a food supply already prepared for their consumption, and generally do not develop outside the body of the host. The parasitic bacteria of importance in sewage originate, in general, in the intestinal tract of human beings and animals and reach the sewage by means of body discharges. Included among the parasitic bacteria are certain specific types which, during their growth within the body of the host, produce toxic or poisonous compounds that cause disease in the host. These bacteria are called *pathogenic bacteria*. They may be present in sewage receiving the body discharges of persons ill with such diseases as typhoid fever, cholera, or other intestinal infections. The possible presence of these microorganisms in sewage is one of the principal reasons why sewage must be carefully collected, adequately treated, disposed of safely, to prevent any transfer by sewage flows of these pathogenic or disease-producing bacteria from person to another.

The *saprophytic bacteria* are those which feed on dead organic matter, thus decomposing organic solids to obtain their needed nourishment, and producing in turn waste substances which consist of both organic and inorganic solids. By this activity they are of utmost importance in sewage treatment methods designed to facilitate or hasten natural decomposition of the organic solids in sewage. Such processes of decomposition will not progress without their activity. In the absence of bacterial life—sterility—decomposition will not take place. Sterile sewage is not subject to the type of decomposition upon which the familiar methods of sewage treatment are based. There are many species of saprophytic bacteria, each of which plays a specific role in the breakdown of the organic solids of sewage. Each species tends to die away following completion of its part in the process of decomposition.

All of the bacteria, parasitic and saprophytic, require, in addition to food, oxygen for respiration. Certain of them can use only oxygen dissolved in water, termed *dissolved oxygen* and sometimes called *free* or *molecular oxygen*. These organisms are known as *aerobic bacteria* and the process of degradation of organic solids which they carry out is terms *aerobic decomposition*, oxidation or decay. This type of decomposition proceeds in the presence of dissolved oxygen without the production of foul odors or unsightly conditions. Other types o9f bacteria cannot exist in the presence of dissolved oxygen but must obtain the required supply of this element from the oxygen content of organic and some inorganic solids which is made available by their decomposition. Such microorganisms are termed *anaerobic bacteria* and the process of degradation of solids which they bring about is called *anaerobic decomposition* or putrefaction, that is, decomposition in the absence of dissolved oxygen, which results in the production of foul odors and unsightly conditions.

To complicate the reactions involved in the decay of organic matter, certain aerobic types can adjust themselves to live and function in the absence of dissolved oxygen and are termed

6

facultative aerobic bacteria. Conversely, some varieties of anaerobic bacteria can become accustomed to live and grow in the presence of dissolved oxygen and are thus termed *facultative anaerobic bacteria*.

Such adaptability of the saprophytic bacteria to various sources of oxygen is of great importance in the decomposition of organic solids in sewage and thus in the various treatment procedures.

In addition to food and oxygen, bacteria require moisture to remain alive. This is adequately provided in sewage by its water component.

In order to function at maximum efficiency, bacteria require a favorable temperature. They are very susceptible to changes in temperature in that their rate of growth and reproduction, which is directly proportional to the amount of work done, is definitely and sharply affected by such variations. The larger proportion of the saprophytic types thrive best at temperatures from 20°C to 40°C, or 68°F to 104°F. These are known as *mesophilic* types. Variations from this temperature range limit the activity of mesophilic bacteria, practically eliminating it at extremely low temperatures and at high temperatures. Mesophilic sludge digestion proceeds most rapidly at 35°C or 95°F. Other bacteria live best at high temperatures, in the range of 55°C to 60°C, or 130°F to 140°F. These are known as *thermophilic* types. Thermophilic bacteria function in sewage treatment, principally in high temperature digestion of sludge solids. A very few types of bacteria find their optimum conditions at low temperatures, 0°C to 5°C, or 32°F to 40°F. These are known as *psychrophilic* bacteria. Temperatures, consequently, are of major importance in the operation of sewage treatment processes.

When all of these environmental conditions of food supply, oxygen, moisture, and temperature are properly maintained at their optimum amounts for the full functioning of the bacteria, decomposition of the sewage solids proceeds in a natural orderly manner.

Other Microscopic Organisms. In addition to the bacteria, other living organisms, usually so small in size as to require microscopic viewing, are found in sewage. They are present in large numbers also, although not in as great densities as the various species of bacteria. These other microorganisms tend to be larger and more complex in structure than the bacteria. Some of them are plants and some are animals. All originate in the soil or in the organic wastes that go to make up sewage. Some are motile (able to move about), others are not. All require food, oxygen, and moisture. They can be either aerobic or anaerobic or facultative in their oxygen requirements. Their growth is affected by the temperature of the environment in much the same degree as the bacteria. These organisms also function in the decomposition and degradation of the organic solids in sewage. They use these solids as food, and produce waste products simpler in chemical structure. These waste products, in turn, frequently serve as food for certain types of saprophytic bacteria. Many of the larger forms are predatory by nature and prey upon other organisms, especially the bacteria.

Macroscopic Organisms: In addition to the two groups of microscopic organisms described above, many larger more complex organisms play a part in the decomposition of organic matter. These are termed *macroscopic*, that is, visible to the naked eye. They include varieties of worms and insects in various stages of development. Some are active in sewage treatment plant facilities and others are prevalent in streams highly polluted by sewage or other organic wastes.

Some forms of all of these organisms, microscopic and macroscopic, are essential to the orderly decomposition of organic matter in nature, and hence are equally essential for the proper functioning of the usual methods of sewage treatment. In fact, biological organisms actually carry on the processes of treatment and the only responsibility of the operator is to provide the environmental condition best suited to them.

Viruses: There is one other form of life found in sewage that is of interest to the sewage treatment plant operator. These are *viruses*. They are smaller than any of the microscopic organisms, too small to be seen under the ordinary microscope used in bacteriological work. They do not play a significant part in sewage treatment processes, but are important in that they are, like pathogenic bacteria, the causative agents of a number of diseases of man. Some, such as the virus of hepatitis, originate in the intestines of man and are carried with intestinal wastes to the sewage.

CONDITION OF SEWAGE

The extent and nature of the bacterial decomposition of solids in sewage has given rise to certain terms descriptive of the condition of the sewage.

Fresh sewage is, as the name indicates, the first stage after waste solids have been added to water to produce sewage. It contains the dissolved oxygen present in the water supply and remains fresh as long as there is sufficient oxygen to maintain aerobic decomposition. Such sewage is turbid with solids in suspension or floating, greyish in color, and has a musty, not unpleasant odor.

Septic sewage describes a sewage in which the dissolved oxygen has been completely exhausted so that anaerobic decomposition of the solids has been established with the production of hydrogen sulfide and other gases. Such sewage is characterized by a blackish color, foul and unpleasant odor, and with black floating and suspended solids.

Stable sewage is sewage in which the solids have decomposed to relative inert solids which are subject to no further decomposition or are only slowly decomposable. Dissolved oxygen is again present by absorption from the atmosphere; there is little or no odor and few suspended solids.

CHEMICAL CHANGES IN SEWAGE COMPOSITION

The activities of biological life in sewage produce many changes in the chemical composition of its solids. These chemical changes or, as they should be called, biochemical changes (since they are brought about by biological growth) not only indicate the activities of the microorganisms but likewise measure the degree of decomposition of the solids and thus the effectiveness of any particular treatment process.

In sewage treatment the physical force of gravity materially reduces the suspended solids in sewage, especially the settleable portion. With the colloidal or non-settleable solids, biochemical changes result in the removal of molecules of water bound in them. This loss of water causes them to stick together or flocculate to form heavier or settleable solids. These settled solids, both organic and inorganic, which are removed are called, respectively, sludge and grit.

Under anaerobic decomposition, oxygen is removed from complex compounds and simpler ones are formed. Such biochemical reactions continue, and step-by-step complex compounds are broken down until the final end product of stable inorganic and organic substances is produced.

The complex organic solids originally added to water to form sewage are compounds of the element *carbon* combined with other elements such as nitrogen, sulfur, phosphorus, hydrogen oxygen, and others, and frequently tightly bound molecules of water. In the process of aerobic decomposition, oxygen is combined with these elements so that the final end products of biochemical change when carried to completion are carbon dioxide, water, nitrates, sulfates, phosphates, and other similar substances usually designated as mineral salts. These are in general quite similar to or the same as the inorganic solids of the sewage and serve as fertilizers or food for the production of new complex organic matter by plant growth.

During the steps of biochemical decomposition, intermediate products are formed. They include organic and inorganic acids, gases such as hydrogen sulfide, methane, carbon dioxide, and in many instances very foul smelling gases resulting from the biochemical changes in organic sulfur compounds. It is these by-products of decomposition which appear in the different stages of sewage treatment, particularly the digestion of sludge solids, and affect, sometimes adversely and sometimes not, the progress of the digestion reactions. The particular compounds produced and the amounts of each are dependent upon the type of microorganisms carrying on the reactions. Thus, the appearance of excessive concentrations of acid in sludge digestion indicates that decomposition of the organic matter is being carried on by organisms that will not produce a rapid and orderly anaerobic destruction of the solids but will cause incomplete digestion and the formation of by-products detrimental to good treatment—such as the production of non-combustible gas which is disagreeably odorous from sludge digestion.

The intermediate products of biochemical decomposition of organic solids provide an excellent indication of the progress of biological activity and the type and degree of treatment resulting.

The process of biochemical changes is well illustrated by the nitrogen, carbon, and sulfur cycles, Figures 2, 3, and 4, which show the steps or stages through which organic matter containing nitrogen, carbon, or sulfur pass from dead organic matter through decomposition to products used by plant life upon which animal life depends. Animal life in turn through waste products, death, and decay ends up as dead organic matter to start the cycles over again.

In all three cycles, the left half of the figures pertain to living matter while the right half of the figures is concerned with dead or waste material. Sewage treatment and disposal lie in the right half.

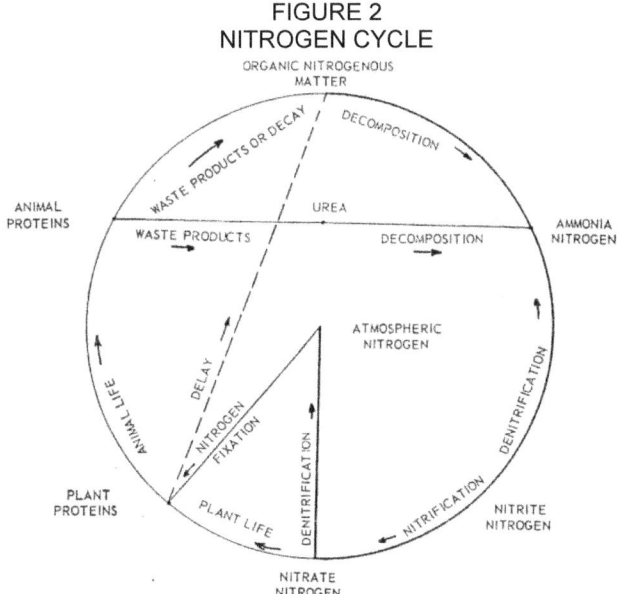

FIGURE 2
NITROGEN CYCLE

9

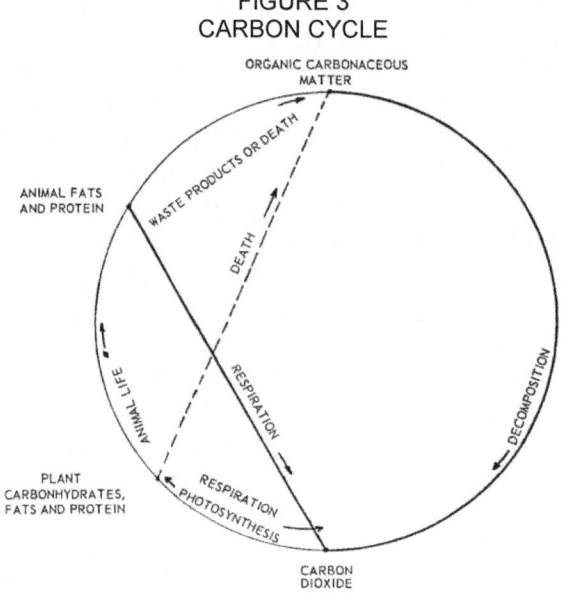

FIGURE 3
CARBON CYCLE

The three cycles illustrate nature's conservation of matter. The products of death are changed to become the support of plant and animal life. Air and water serve as a huge reservoir in which oxygen, nitrogen, carbon dioxide, and other gases produced in one part of the cycle can be stored till needed in another part.

Sewage treatment does not alter or modify natural processes. A treatment plant is merely a device to localize in a most suitable place a workshop in which the natural processes of decomposition of dead organic matter can be carried on as far as necessary and to some extent be controlled and accelerated.

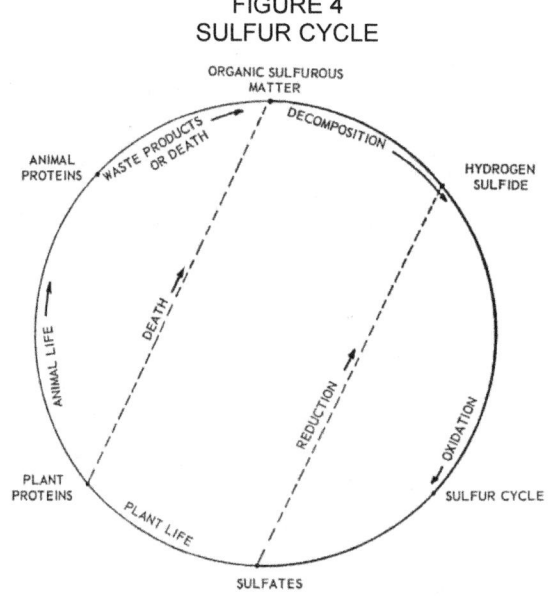

FIGURE 4
SULFUR CYCLE

10

In the biochemical changes in sewage, the dissolved gases play an important role. This is especially true of dissolved oxygen which, when present in the sewage or when added to it by treatment devices, insures the growth and activities of the aerobic microorganisms and thus the progress of aerobic decomposition without the production of putrefactive conditions. When dissolved oxygen is completely exhausted, the aerobic organisms are displaced by anaerobic varieties, and anaerobic decomposition takes place with the rapid development of putrefaction and the accompanying unsightly black appearance of the sewage together with foul odors. Although the other gases dissolved in the water fraction of the sewage do not control biological activities to the extent of the dissolved oxygen, they also play a part. Hydrogen sulfide, a foul-smelling gas, is the result of anaerobic decomposition of sulfur-bearing compounds and produces acid conditions which may affect further biochemical reactions and which will exert corrosive action on the sewage structures. Carbon dioxide, if present in excessive amounts, indicates that acid decomposition of the solids is taking place, with resulting reduction in the rate of decay. In the case of sludge digestion, carbon dioxide production reduces the generation of combustible gas which is a valuable by-product of such operations.

The chemical or biochemical changes in sewage solids are best measured by chemical analyses. Such chemical analyses will:

1. Detect and measure biochemical reactions.
2. Detect and measure the chemical compounds formed during such biochemical reactions.
3. Measure the degree and rate of the decomposition of organic solids.
4. Measure the efficiencies of various methods and devices used in sewage treatment.

CHAPTER 2

SEWAGE DISPOSAL

As discussed in Chapter 1, sewage is the waste water of community life. In composition it includes dissolved and suspended organic solids, which are putrescible and, therefore, will decay. Sewage also contains countless numbers of living organisms—bacteria and other microorganisms whose life activities cause the process of decomposition. When decay proceeds under anaerobic conditions, that is, in the absence of dissolved oxygen in the sewage, offensive conditions result and odors and unsightly appearances are produced. When decay proceeds under aerobic conditions, that is, in the presence of dissolved oxygen, offensive conditions do not result and the process is greatly accelerated.

The promotion of cleanliness by the removal of filth and wastes to an area remote from the center of activity is important. It is only by such practices that the environment can be maintained in an acceptable and safe condition. Among the waste products of life are the disease-producing (pathogenic) bacteria and viruses which can be readily transferred by sewage from sick individuals to well ones. Properly regulated procedures for disposal of sewage are necessary to protect the health of the people and to maintain the cleanliness of the environment and the comfort of the inhabitants.

A sharp distinction must be made between the term "sewage disposal" which is the subject of this chapter and "sewage treatment" which is covered in subsequent chapters. All sewage has to be disposed of. Some sewage is subjected to various types of treatment *before* disposal, but some sewage receives no treatment before disposal.

SEWAGE TREATMENT

Sewage treatment is a process in which the solids in sewage are partially removed and partially changed by decomposition from complex highly putrescible organic solids to mineral or relatively stable organic solids. The extent of this change is dependent on the treatment processes involved. After all treatment processes have been completed, it is still necessary to dispose of the liquid and the solids which have been removed.

SEWAGE DISPOSAL

There are three methods by which final disposal of sewage can be accomplished.

Disposal by Irrigation: This involves spreading the sewage over the surface of the ground, generally by irrigation ditches. There is some evaporation, but most of the sewage soaks into the ground and supplies moisture with small amounts of fertilizing ingredients for plant life. Use of this method is largely restricted to small volumes of sewage from a relatively small population and where land area is available. It has its best use in arid or semi-arid areas where the moisture added to the soil is of special value. If crops are cultivated on the disposal area, industrial wastes which would be toxic or impair the growth of vegetation must be excluded from sewers. Because of the ever present possibility that sewage may contain pathogenic organisms, the production of foods for human consumption which may be eaten without cooking is not desirable.

Subsurface Disposal: By this method sewage is introduced into the ground below its surface through pits or tile fields. It is commonly used for disposal of settled sewage from residences or institutions where there is only a limited volume of sewage. Because it has little application for municipalities, any discussion of the many details involved would be of little value in this manual.

Disposal by Dilution: Disposal by dilution is the simple method of discharging sewage into a surface water such as a river, lake, or ocean. This results in the pollution of the receiving water. The degree of pollution depends on the dilution, the volume, and composition of sewage as compared to the volume of water with which it is mixed. When the volume and organic content of the sewage is small, compared with the volume of the receiving water, the dissolved oxygen present in the receiving water is adequate to provide for aerobic decomposition of the organic solids in the sewage so that nuisance conditions do not develop. However, in spite of the continued aerobic status of the receiving water, the bacterial pollution remains a health menace and floating solids in the sewage, if not previously removed, are visible evidence of the pollution.

Where the dissolved oxygen in the receiving water is inadequate to maintain aerobic decomposition, anaerobic decomposition takes place and putrefaction with objectionable conditions results. It is not so much the volume of sewage that is the critical factor as the amount of readily decomposable organic matter in the sewage. Thus, a volume of sewage that has been treated to remove or reduce this organic matter can be discharged to a natural surface water without creating objectionable conditions, while the same volume of raw or untreated sewage might produce a nuisance. The dissolved oxygen in the receiving water is the determining factor.

ROLE OF DISSOLVED OXYGEN IN RECEIVING WATERS

When sewage solids are discharged into water, decay and decomposition proceed owing to activities of the bacteria and microorganisms present in the sewage and in the receiving water. Oxygen is required for the functioning of all such biological and biochemical reactions. As discussed previously, when dissolved oxygen is present, aerobic organisms carry on the work, and aerobic decomposition of the organic solids proceeds. When oxygen is absent, anaerobic organisms take over and putrefaction results. Thus, when sewage is discharged into a stream, the reactions depend upon the dissolved oxygen present in the water.

Oxygen is dissolved in water from air in contact with the water surface until the point of saturation at a given temperature is reached. At a temperature of 0°C, water contains 14.6 ppm of dissolved oxygen at saturation. This concentration is reduced as the water temperature increases, so that at a temperature of 15°C, the dissolved oxygen concentration at saturation is 10.00 ppm. When the dissolved oxygen concentration is reduced below the saturation value, more is dissolved from the air. Turbulent flow of a stream over stones, riffles, and rapids increase the rate of solution of oxygen, or reaeration. By means of reaeration, additional oxygen is made available for the biochemical decomposition of putrescible organic solids

BIOCHEMICAL OXYGEN DEMAND – BOD

The amount of oxygen required for the aerobic biological oxidation of the organic solids in a sewage or waste is the *biochemical oxygen demand (BOD)*. It is determined by a laboratory test. Since this decomposition extends over a long period of time and is dependent on temperature, BOD values from laboratory tests should state the time and temperature used in making the test. Those most commonly used are 5 days and 20°C (68°F); and unless other time and temperature are specifically mentioned, these are generally assumed to have been the time and temperature used.

13

SELF-PURIFICATION

When sewage is discharged into a stream, decay and decomposition continue and proceed towards completion. A stream polluted at a given point would, as a result of the decomposition of the polluting organic matter, tend to return to a state similar to that before the pollution occurred. This is generally designated as the process of *self-purification*. It proceeds by physical, chemical, and biological means. The physical reactions are essentially those of sedimentation of suspended solids to form deposits called sludge banks, the bleaching and other effects of sunlight and reaeration.

The chemical and biological reactions are more complex. Here the living organisms feed on the organic solids, producing waste products which may destroy them and at the same time serve as food for succeeding types, which carry on the process of decomposition to a further degree—until finally the complex organic compounds are reduced to stable inorganic salts, such as nitrates, sulfates, phosphates, etc. These, in turn, serve as food for other biological forms, such as the algae, which during the process of their growth and metabolism produce oxygen as a waste product. This then dissolves in the water, adding to that obtained through reaeration. These reactions return the stream or water to a condition of relative cleanliness, and self-purification may be considered complete. The progress of self-purification is dependent upon time, temperature, oxygen supply, and the other environmental factors which regulate biological growths.

Self-purification of a stream is generally considered to take place in four stages with the stream divided into four zones which merge into each other. These are called the zones of degradation, decomposition, recovery, and clean water. As noted below under zone of decomposition, this zone is not always present.

Zone of Degradation: The first of these zones occurs immediately below the point of pollution and is designated as the *Zone of Degradation*. This zone is characterized by visible evidences of pollution. Floating solids, such as bits of garbage, sticks, paper, and possibly fecal solids, are present. The turbidity of the stream is markedly increased by the sewage discharge. Oxygen is reduced but is not immediately exhausted. Fish life decreases and is limited to those species which can survive in water with relatively little dissolved oxygen. Biological life, although not visible, abounds. Bacteria are present in large numbers—including those pathogenic ones that were in the sewage. Fungus organisms also are present and in time long stringy growths of these will be found clinging to rocks and shrubs on the shoreline. Active growth of the microbiological life absorbs and gradually exhausts the dissolved oxygen. If the flow in the stream in this section is slow, sedimentation of the suspended solids takes place to create sludge banks. This accumulation of sewage solids putrefies and further contributes to the degradation of the stream.

Zone of Decomposition: As the dissolved oxygen supply is exhausted, the *Zone of Degradation* passes into the *Zone of Decomposition*, where anaerobic decomposition or putrefaction is initiated.

With a heavy load of pollution this occurs quickly. With a smaller discharge of sewage relative to the volume of the stream, the change to the second zoned proceeds more slowly. When the volume of sewage discharged is relatively very small so that dissolved oxygen is continuously adequate to sustain aerobic life, the stream may not pass into the *Zone of Decomposition*, and the *Zone of Degradation* may pass directly into the *Zone of Recovery*.

The *Zone of Decomposition* is characterized by the development of anaerobic decomposition. Dissolved oxygen is almost or entirely depleted and all fish life disappears. The water turns black, and foul odors are produced as a result of the decomposition of the organic solids by anaerobic organisms which are present in large numbers. Sedimentation of suspended solids continues with sludge deposits appearing which are similar to those occurring in the first zone. As decomposition of organic matter progresses, the putrescible solids are reduced in amount and putrefactive reactions begin to decline in rate. Oxygen from reaeration first equals and then exceeds the rate at which it is being used for biochemical decomposition so that some dissolved oxygen is present at the lower edge of this zone, which merges into the third zone, the *Zone of Recovery*.

Zone of Recovery: In the *Zone of Recovery*, dissolved oxygen appears in gradually increasing amounts, organic solids decrease, and a favorable appearance of the stream is attained. Microorganisms in reduced numbers are present but the anaerobes are dying and aerobic species are present. Fish can again survive, and other higher forms of organisms appear in large numbers. Sedimentation of solids continues, and the organic solids in the sludge banks and bottom deposits are acted on by worms and larvae which are large enough to be visible, to affect further decomposition.

As previously indicated, if aerobic conditions are always present in the stream, the *Zone of Recovery* follows immediately after the *Zone of Degradation*.

Zone of Clean Water. In the *Zone of Recovery*, decomposition of organic solids is largely completed and mineral and stable inorganic solids are found in major concentrations. The stream then flows into the fourth and final zone, the *Zone of Clean Water*. Here the water is similar in appearance to what it was before it received the polluting material. Visible floating solids are absent, the water is clear, free from suspended matter, and has returned to its original color. Oxygen is at or near the point of saturation. Living microscopic organisms, including bacteria, are present but in relatively small numbers. Larger organisms are abundant, principally the algae and other forms which find in clean water their optimum environment and which use as food the stable inorganic compounds resulting from decomposition of the complex organic solids characteristic of the sewage that produced the pollution. Fish are generally more abundant than before the pollution occurred because of the increase in the population of macroscopic organisms which serves to increase the food supply for the fish.

The time required for self-purification of a stream or the distance it must flow to pass through the four zones is dependent upon the strength and relative volumes of pollution and stream flow, on the turbulence of flow, the temperature of the water, and, of major importance, on whether or not additional pollution is discharged into the stream during the progress of self-purification.

Possibility of Residual Pollution: The process of self-purification affects primarily the putrescible matter in the sewage. Some pathogenic organisms and viruses may survive. Other polluting substances, especially metallic and other compounds not completely organic in nature originating from industrial and manufacturing processes, are not changed by the biochemical processes. These substances, if present in sufficient concentration, interfere with and inhibit biological decomposition and may remain as a residual pollution which can impair the quality of the receiving stream to such a degree that the water is not suitable for use for water supply, recreational, industrial, and other purposes.

NEED FOR SEWAGE TREATMENT

The problem of sewage disposal developed with the use of water to pick up and carry away waste products of human life. Prior to that the volume of wastes, without the water vehicle, was small and disposal was largely restricted to the individual's or family's excreta. The earliest method was to leave body waste and garbage on the surface of the ground where it was gradually decayed by bacteria, mostly the saprophytic anaerobic type. This caused the production of foul odors. Later experience showed that if these wastes were promptly buried the development of these odors was prevented. The next step was the development of the earth privy, a method for the disposal of excremental wastes which is still widely used.

With the development of community water supplies and the use of water to flush or transport wastes from habitations, it became necessary to find disposal methods not only for the wastes themselves but for the water which carried them. All of the three possible methods—irrigation, subsurface disposal and dilution—were employed.

As urban communities increased in population, with proportional increase in the volume of sewage and amount of organic waste, all methods of disposal resulted in such unsatisfactory conditions that remedial measures became essential and the development of methods of treatment of sewage prior to ultimate disposal was started.

The objectives sought in sewage treatment include:

1. Maintenance of sources for use as domestic water supplies
2. Prevention of disease
3. Prevention of nuisances
4. Maintenance of clean waters for bathing and other recreational purposes
5. Maintenance of clean waters for the propagation and survival of fish life
6. Conservation of water for industrial and agricultural uses
7. Prevention of silting in navigable channels

A sewage treatment plant is designed to remove from the sewage enough organic and inorganic solids so that it can be disposed of without infringing upon the objectives sought.

The various processes used in sewage treatment parallel closely the processes involved in the self-purification of a polluted stream. Treatment devices merely localize and confine these processes to a restricted, controlled, suitable area and provide favorable conditions for the acceleration of the physical and biochemical reactions.

The extent or degree of treatment needed varies greatly from place to place. Basically there are three determining factors:

1. The character and amount of the solids carried by the sewage
2. The objectives sought
3. The ability or capacity of the land (in disposal by irrigation and subsurface disposal) or the receiving water (in disposal by dilution) to handle by self-purification or dispersal the water and solids in the sewage without infringing on the objectives sought

The removal of floating solids by screens may be adequate for sewage discharged into coastal sea waters. A very high removal of suspended solids, decomposition of dissolved organic solids and destruction of pathogenic organisms may be required, however, before discharge to a river which is used downstream as a source of public water supply. Adequate treatment prior to disposal to attain objectives is becoming a must, but excessive overtreatment is an unwarranted extravagance.

After the disposal of the sewage effluent from a treatment plant, there still remain in the plant the solids and water constituting the sludge which has been removed from the sewage. This, too, must be disposed of safely and without nuisance.

The progress of self-purification of a stream can be measured by appropriate physical, chemical, and biological laboratory tests. Similar tests are used to measure and control the progress of sewage treatment plant processes.

LEGAL ASPECTS OF SEWAGE DISPOSAL

The serious problem involving the disposal of sewage and other wastes by adequate and effective means that will eliminate nuisances and not violate the rights and welfare of individuals and communities has led to the development of laws and regulations governing such disposal.

It is presumed that in ancient times, customs slowly developed which regulated the disposal of the wastes of the individuals and of the group. As time went on, custom took on the force of law, and led, over the years, to the formulation of legal regulations—first as common law and then as statutory law.

Mosaic Law: One of the earliest recorded regulations pertaining to waste disposal can be found in the 23rd chapter of Deuteronomy. Moses, as the leader of a great community of people, found it necessary to establish rules for the conduct of his followers. Verses 12 to 14 of this chapter contain that portion of the Mosaic Law which placed the responsibility for proper disposal of excrement with the individual and required that it be buried. Modern research has not changed the fundamental principles involved. Increased knowledge of the transmission of disease from man to man and the need for personal cleanliness in community life have led to better practices and regulation for disposal of these waste products.

Common Law: Perhaps the earliest regulations related to sewage disposal and water pollution were based on the common law as related to the use of streams by owners of property bordering the stream. These specified (a) that every riparian owner is entitled to reasonable use of the water flowing past his property, and (b) that every riparian owner is entitled to have the waters of the stream reach his property in their natural condition and unimpaired as to quality and quantity.

Modern Legal Practice: The general principles of Common Law have been further clarified and modified by any specific statutory laws and regulations concerned with the disposal of sewage into streams and other bodies of water. Large numbers of lawsuits based on instances of pollution have led to legislation in most states governing the treatment and disposal of community wastes. Such legislation usually applies not only to pollution of waterways but controls the installation of treatment facilities by requiring approval of design and supervision of operation by some government body. Disposal of industrial waste as well as of domestic sewage is included in the legislation.

New York State now has stringent laws relating to this important matter of sewage and wastes disposal. Articles 11 and 12 of the Public Health Law regulate sewage disposal for the prevention and control of water pollution.

Article 11, Title III, prohibits the discharge of sewage into waters of the State unless a permit for such discharge has been granted by the State Commissioner of Health. The legal procedures for the control of pollution and regulations relative to construction of sewers and sewage treatment facilities are included.

Article 12 is concerned with the control of water pollution. Section 1200 outlines the policy of the State in this regard, and Section 1201 states the purpose of these regulations.

"Section 1200. Declaration of Policy. It is declared to be the public policy of the State of New York to maintain reasonable standards of purity of the waters of the state consistent with public health and public enjoyment thereof, the propagation and protection of fish and wild life, including birds, mammals, and other terrestrial and aquatic life, and the industrial development of the State, and to that end require the use of all known available and reasonable methods to prevent and control the pollution of the waters of the State of New York."

"Section 1201. Statement of Purpose. It is the purpose of this article to safeguard the waters of the State from pollution by: (a) preventing any new pollution, and (b) abating polluting existing when this chapter is enacted, under a program consistent with the declaration of policy above stated in the provisions of this article."

The ensuing sections of the New York State Public Health Law delineate the procedures that must be followed to control pollution of the State's water resources. The principle of classification of the surface and ground water resources of the State in accordance with the usage to which a specific water should be put is established. Various degrees of permissible pollution of streams, lakes, and ground waters are recognized.

In 1950, there were established seven classes of standards for fresh surface waters, four for tidal salt waters and two for ground waters. Several others have subsequently been established to meet special local conditions. The classes are based on the best use of the waters. The standards do not specify the character of polluting material discharged but are those which the waters must meet after such material has had an opportunity for reasonable dilution and mixture with the waters. Indirectly, however, this does not indicate the treatment pollutional material must have prior to discharge.

Best usages include use for drinking, culinary, food processing, bathing, fishing, ariculture, production of shellfish for marketing, agriculture and industry, navigation, sewage and wastes disposal.

Laws and regulations governing pollution and sewage disposal have become more and more essential with population increase. Only by such legal procedures and their enforcement can a clean, comfortable, and healthy environment be assured for all people.

CHAPTER 3

SEWAGE TREATMENT METHODS

Satisfactory disposal of sewage, whether by irrigation, subsurface methods or dilution, is dependent on its treatment prior to disposal. For disposal by dilution, adequate treatment is necessary to prevent contamination of receiving waters to a degree which might interfere with their best use, whether it be for water supply, recreation, fishing, or any other required purpose. Even when a body of water has no other use than for the disposal of sewage or liquid industrial wastes, some treatment is necessary to avoid offensive conditions.

Sewage treatment is a means whereby in a limit4ed segregated area, and under controlled conditions, it is possible to carry out the various stages, described in Chapter 2, as taking pace in the self-purification of a stream.

The purpose of sewage treatment prior to disposal is to remove from the sewage enough solids to permit the remainder to be discharged to receiving waters without interfering with its best or proper use, taking into consideration the capacity of the receiving waters to assimilate the added load. The solids which are removed are primarily organic but include also inorganic solids. As the best use of a receiving water may vary from use of the water for drinking and culinary purposes to use, primarily, for the disposal of sewage and industrial wastes, the amount or degree of treatment provided for the sewage or wastes must be varied accordingly. Treatment must be provided for the solids and liquids which are removed as sludge, and treatment to control odors, to retard biological activity or destroy pathogenic organisms may also be needed.

While the devices used in sewage treatment are numerous, they may all be included under five methods:

1. Preliminary treatment
2. Primary treatment
3. Secondary treatment
4. Chlorination
5. Sludge treatment

PRELIMINARY TREATMENT

At most plants preliminary treatment is used to protect pumping equipment and facilitate subsequent treatment processes. Preliminary devices are designed to remove or cut up the larger suspended and floating solids; to remove the heavy inorganic solids; and to remove excessive amounts of oils or greases. In some few instances where, for example, disposal by dilution is into tidal waters, the results accomplished by preliminary treatment may be adequate.

To effect the objectives of preliminary treatment, the following devices are commonly used:

1. Screens—rack, bar or fine
2. Comminuting devices—grinders, cutters, shredders
3. Grit chambers
4. Pre-aeration tanks

19

In addition to the above, chlorination may be used in preliminary treatment. Since chlorination may be used at all stages in treatment, it is considered to be a method by itself and is covered in a separate section in this Manual.

Preliminary treatment devices require careful design and operation. Detailed discussion of them is contained in Chapter 4.

PRIMARY TREATMENT

By this treatment most of the settleable solids or about 40 to 60 percent of the suspended solids are separated or removed from the sewage by the physical process of sedimentation in settling tanks. When certain chemicals are used with primary tanks, much of the colloidal as well as the settleable solids or a total of 80 to 90 percent of the suspended solids are removed. Biological activity in the sewage is of negligible importance.

The purpose of primary devices is to reduce the velocity of the sewage sufficiently to permit solids to settle. Therefore, primary devices may be called settling tanks. Because of variations in design and operation, settling tanks can be divided into four general groups:

1. Septic tanks
2. Two story tanks—Imhoff and several patented units
3. Plain sedimentation tank with mechanical sludge removal
4. Upward flow clarifiers with mechanical sludge removal

When chemicals are used, other auxiliary units are employed. These are:

1. Chemical feed units
2. Mixing devices
3. Flocculators

The results obtained by primary treatment, together with anaerobic sludge digestion as described later, are such that they can be compared with the zone of degradation in stream self-purification. The use of chlorine with primary treatment is discussed under the section on Chlorination.

In many cases, primary treatment is adequate to permit the discharge of the effluent to the receiving waters without interfering with the proper subsequent uses of the waters.

SECONDARY TREATMENT

This must be used where sewage after primary treatment still contains more organic solids in suspension or solution than the receiving waters can assimilate without infringing upon their normal proper use. Secondary treatment depends primarily upon biological aerobic organisms for the biochemical decomposition of organic solids to inorganic or stable organic solids. It is comparable to the zone of recovery in the self-purification of a stream.

The devices used in secondary treatment may be divided into our groups:

1. Trickling filters with secondary settling tanks
2. Aeration tanks—(a) activated sludge with final settling tanks, and (b) contact aeration
3. Intermittent sand filters
4. Stabilization ponds

The use of chlorine with secondary treatment is discussed under the chapter on Chlorination.

CHLORINATION

This is a method of treatment which may be employed for many purposes in all stages in sewage treatment, and even prior to preliminary treatment. It involves the application of chlorine to the sewage for the following purposes:

1. Disinfection or destruction of pathogenic organisms
2. Prevention of sewage decomposition—(a) odor control, (b) protection of plant structures
3. Aid in plant operation—(a) sedimentation, (b) trickling filters, (c) activated sludge bulking
4. Reduction or delay of biochemical oxygen demand

SLUDGE TREATMENT

The solids removed from sewage in both primary and secondary treatment units, together with the water removed with them, constitute sewage sludge. While in some few instances satisfactory disposal without treatment is practical, it is generally necessary to subject sludge to some treatment to prepare or condition it for disposal without creating unsatisfactory conditions. Such treatment has two objectives—the removal of part or all of the water in the sludge to greatly reduce its volume, and the decomposition of the putrescible organic solids to mineral solids or to relatively stable organic solids. This is accomplished by a combination of two or more of the following methods.

1. Thickening
2. Digestion with or without heat
3. Drying on sand bed—open or covered
4. Conditioning with chemicals
5. Elutriation
6. Vacuum filtration
7. Heat drying
8. Incineration
9. Wet oxidation
10. Floatation with chemicals and air
11. Centrifuging

PACKAGE UNITS

The term "package units" has come into quite common use in recent years to describe equipment which has been put on the market by a number of manufacturers. There is no universally accepted definition of the term. One meaning is a complete installation including both mechanisms and pre-fabricated containers. This term is also applied to installations where only the mechanisms are purchased and the containers constructed by the purchaser in accordance with plans and specifications prepared by the manufacturer. The latter appears to be the more generally accepted interpretation.

Though specific limitations have not been established, individual package units have, in general, been small installations serving a limited population.

Package units have been adapted to practically all the treatment devices, either singly or in various combinations, listed in this chapter.

CHAPTER 4

PRELIMINARY TREATMENT

The purpose of preliminary treatment is to remove from the sewage some of its constituents which can clog or damage pumps, or interfere with subsequent treatment processes. Preliminary treatment devices are, therefore, designed to:

1. Remove or reduce in size the large suspended or floating organic solids. These solids consist of pieces of wood, cloth, paper, garbage, together with some fecal matter.
2. Remove heavy inorganic solids such as sand, gravel, and possible metallic objects, all of which are called grit.
3. Remove excessive amounts of oils or greases.

A number of devices or types of equipment are used to obtain these objectives.

RACKS AND BAR SCREENS

These consist of bars usually spaced three-quarter inches to six inches. Those most commonly used provide clear openings of one to two inches. Although large screens are sometimes set vertically, screens are usually set at an angle of 45 to 60 degrees with the vertical. They may be cleaned either manually or by means of automatically operated rakes. It has been recommended that hand-cleaned screens, except those for emergency use, should be placed on slopes of 30 to 45 degrees with the vertical. The solids removed by these units can be disposed of by burial or incineration or they may be reduced in size by grinders or shredding devices and returned to the sewage.

FINE SCREENS

Screens with openings of one-eighth inch or less have been used in sewage treatment. They can be classified as bandscreens, disk screens, and drum screens, and are mentioned here because there are a few in operation at existing sewage treatment plants in New York State. They are commonly used in the treatment of many types of industrial wastes, but are no longer considered for sewage treatment except in special cases, because of the limited results obtained.

COMMINUTING DEVICES

Grinders, Cutters, and Shredders: These are devices to break or cut up solids to such size that they can be returned to the sewage without danger of clogging pumps or piping or affecting subsequent treatment devices. They may be separate devices to grind solids removed by screens or a combination of screen and cutters installed within the sewage flow without actually removing these larger solids from the sewage. These latter devices are made by a number of manufacturers under various trade names and, in most cases, consist of fixed, rotating, or oscillating teeth or blades, acting together to reduce the solids to a size which will pass through fixed or rotating screens or grids having openings of about one-fourth inch. Some of these devices are even designed to operate as a low-lift pump.

GRIT CHAMBERS

Sewage usually contains a relatively large amount of inorganic solids such as sand, cinders, and gravel which are called grit. The amount varies greatly depending on a number of factors, but primarily on whether the collecting sewer system is of the sanitary or combined type. Grit will damage pumps by abrasion and cause serious operation difficulties in sedimentation tanks and with sludge digestion by accumulation around and plugging of outlets. It is, therefore, common practice to remove this material by grit chambers. They are usually located ahead of pumps or comminuting devices, and if mechanically cleaned as described below, should be preceded by coarse bar rack screens. Grit chambers are generally designed as long channels. In these channels, the velocity is reduced sufficiently to deposit heavy inorganic solids but to retain organic material in suspension. Channel type chambers should be designed to provide controlled velocities as close as possible to 1.0 foot per second. The detention period should be based on size of particle to be removed and is usually between 20 seconds and 1.0 minute. This is attained by providing several chambers to accommodate variation in flow or by proportional weirs at the end of the chamber or other flow control devices which permit regulation of flow velocity. There are also patented devices to remove grit. A recent development is the injection of air several feet above the floor of a tank type unit. The rolling action of the air keeps the lighter organic matter in suspension and allows the grit relatively free from organic matter to be deposited in the quiescent zone beneath the zone of air diffusion.

Cleaning: Grit chambers are designed to be cleaned manually or by mechanically operated devices. If cleaned manually, storage space for the deposited grit is usually provided. Grit chambers for plants treating wastes from combined sewers should have at least two hand-cleaned units or a mechanically cleaned unit with by-pass. Mechanically cleaned grit chambers are recommended. Single hand-cleaned chambers with by-pass are acceptable for small sewage treatment plants serving sanitary sewer systems. Chambers other than channel type are acceptable, if provided with adequate and flexible controls for agitation and/or air supply devices and with grit removal equipment.

There are a number of mechanical cleaning units available which remove grit by scrapers or buckets while the grit chamber is in normal operation. These require much less grit storage space than manually operated units.

Washing Grit: Grit always contains some organic matter which decomposes and creates odors. To facilitate economical disposal of grit without causing nuisance, the organic matter is sometimes washed from the grit and returned to the sewage. Special equipment is available to wash grit. Mechanical cleaning equipment generally provides for washing grit with sewage as it is removed from the chamber.

Quantity of Grit: This depends on the type of tributary sewer system, the condition of the sewer lines, and other factors. Strictly domestic sewage collected in well-constructed sewers will contain little grit, while combined sewage will carry large volumes of grit reaching a peak at times of severe storms. In general, 1.0 to 4.0 cu. ft. of grit per million gallons can be expected.

Operation: Manually cleaned grit chambers for combined sewage should be cleaned after every large storm. Under ordinary conditions these grit chambers should be cleaned when the deposited grit has filled 50 to 60 percent of the grit storage space. This should be tested at least every ten days.

When mechanically cleaned chambers are used, they must be cleaned at regular intervals to prevent undue load on the cleaning mechanism. Recommendations of the manufacturer should be rigidly observed. This plus experience will determine the cleaning schedule.

A grit in which marked odors develop indicates that too much organic matter is being removed in the grit chamber. If sludge from settling tank is excessively high in inorganic matter, or if there is excessive wear in pumps, comminutors, sludge collectors, or other mechanical equipment, the reason is likely to be inefficient functioning of the grit chamber in removing grit and a study of this unit should be made.

Disposal of Screenings and Grit: Screenings decompose rapidly with foul odors. They should be kept covered in cans at the screens and removed at least daily or oftener for disposal by burial, incineration or through grinders. The walls and platforms of the screen chamber and screen itself should be hosed down and kept clean. Grit containing much organic matter may have to be buried to prevent odor nuisances.

PRE-AERATION TANKS

Pre-aeration of sewage, that is aeration before primary treatment, is sometimes provided for the following purposes:

1. To obtain a greater removal of suspended solids in sedimentation tanks
2. To assist in the removal of grease and oil carried in the sewage
3. To freshen up septic sewage prior to further treatment
4. BOD Reduction

Pre-aeration is accomplished by introducing air into the sewage for a period of 20 to 30 minutes at the design flow. This may be accomplished by forcing compressed air into the sewage at a rate usually taken as 0.10 cu. ft. per gallon of sewage when 30 minutes of aeration is provided or by mechanical agitation whereby the sewage is stirred or agitated so that new surfaces are continually brought into contact with the atmosphere for absorption of air. To insure proper agitation when compressed air is forced into the sewage, air is usually supplied at the rate of 1.0 to 4.0 cubic feet per minute per linear foot of tank or channel. When air for mechanical agitation (either with or without the use of chemicals) is used for additional purpose of obtaining increased reduction in BOD, the detention period should be at least 45 minutes at design flow. The agitation of sewage in the presence of air tends to collect or flocculate lighter suspended solids into heavier masses which settle more readily in the sedimentation tanks. It also helps to separate grease and oil from the sewage and sewage solids and to carry them to the surface. By the addition of air, aerobic conditions are also restored in septic sewage to improve subsequent treatment.

The devices and equipment for introducing the air into the sewage are the same or similar to those used in the activated sludge process and are described under that heading in Chapter 6.

CHAPTER 5

PRIMARY TREATMENT

Primary treatment devices are designed to remove from the sewage organic and inorganic settleable solids by the physical process of sedimentation. This is effected by reducing the velocity of flow. Sewers are designed to maintain a velocity of about two feet per second, which is adequate to carry all solids with the sewage flow and prevent their deposition in the sewers. In preliminary treatment this velocity is lowered to about one foot per second for a very brief period during which the heavier inorganic solids are settled out as grit. In primary treatment the velocity of flow is reduced to a fraction of an inch per second in a settling or sedimentation tank for sufficient time to allow the major portion of the settleable solids, which are largely organic, to settle out of the sewage flow.

Principle primary treatment devices are sedimentation tanks, some of which have the further function of providing for the decomposition of the settled organic solids, known as sludge digestion. There are a number of types of tanks used.

SEPTIC TANKS

The septic tank was one of the earliest primary treatment devices developed. It is designed to hold the sewage at a very low velocity under anaerobic conditions for a period of 12 to 24 hours during which a high removal of the settleable solids in the sewage is effected. These solids decompose in the bottom of the tank with the formation of gas which, entrained in the solids, causes them to rise through the sewage to the surface and lie as a scum layer until the gas has escaped, after which they again settle. This continual floatation and resettling of solids carry them in the current of the sewage toward the outlet, with some eventually passing out with the effluent, thus partially defeating the purpose of the tank. Due to the long holding period and the mixing with decomposing solids, the sewage itself leaves the tank in a septic condition difficult to treat in secondary units.

Septic tanks are no longer used except for very small installations. They do, however, have common use for individual residences, small institutions or schools where the tank effluent can be disposed of by sub-surface methods or where the dilution factor in the receiving waters is high. In such situations, they have the value of requiring a minimum of attention to operation which involves only occasional cleaning of the tank of sludge and scum accumulations.

FIGURE 5
SEPTIC TANK

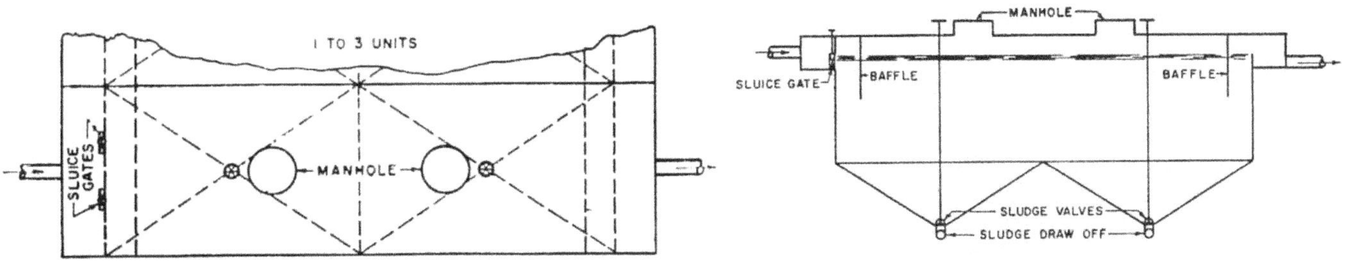

TWO-STORY TANKS

The two-story tank was developed to correct the two main defects of the septic tank.

1. It prevents the solids once removed from the sewage from again being mixed with it though still providing for decomposition of these solids in the same unit, and
2. It provides an effluent amenable to further treatment

Contact between the sewage and the anaerobic digesting sludge is practically eliminated and the holding period in the tank is reduced.

The best known and most used two-story tank was originally designed by Dr. Karl Imhoff and is known as the Imhoff tank. It may be either circular or rectangular and is divided into three compartments or chambers—(1) the upper section, called the flowing through chamber or sedimentation compartment; (2) the lower section known as sludge digestion chamber; and (3) the gas vent and scum chamber. Figure 6 shows a typical plan and cross-section of an Imhoff tank. It is desirable to be able to reverse the direction of flow to prevent excessive deposition of solids at one end of the flowing-through chamber. Reversing the flow every month will result in an even accumulation of sludge across the bottom of the tank.

FIGURE 6
IMHOFF TANK

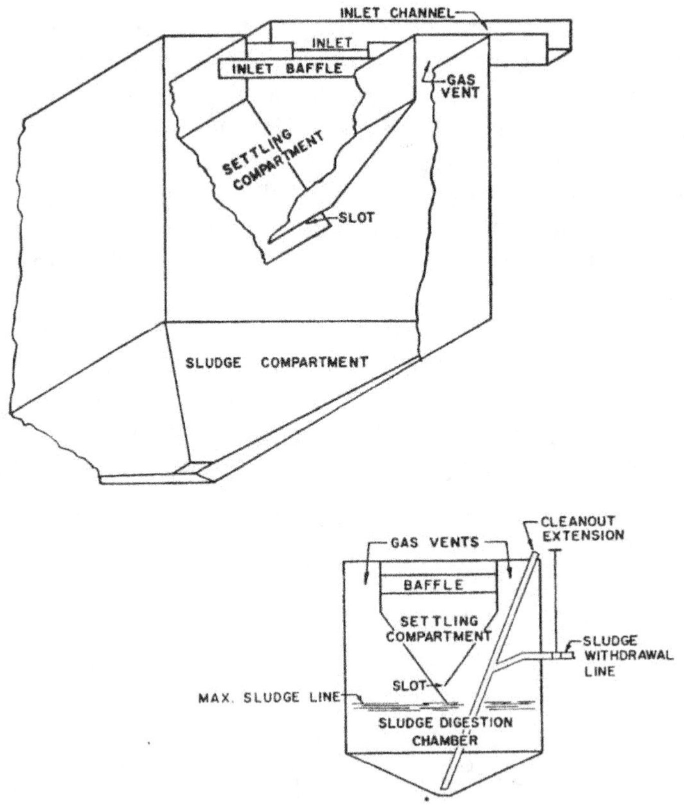

In operation, all of the sewage flows through the upper compartment. Solids settle to the bottom of this compartment, which has slopes of about 1.4 vertical to one horizontal, slide down and pass through an opening or slot at the bottom. One of the bottom slopes extends at least six inches beyond the slot. This forms a trap to prevent gas or digesting sludge particles in the lower section from entering the sewage in the upper section. The gas and any rising sludge

26

particles are diverted to the gas vent and scum chamber. This eliminates the main disadvantage of the septic tank. The gas vents should have a surface area of at least 20 percent of the total area of the tank.

It is desirable to start the operation of an Imhoff tank in the spring or early summer when the temperature in the sludge compartment is high enough to promote rapid digestion. Seeding the tank with actively digesting sludge from a nearby Imhoff tank or separate sludge digester is advisable if it can be done conveniently. Otherwise the pH of the sludge in the sludge compartment should be controlled and maintained above 6.8 to prevent an acid condition unfavorable for proper digestion. This can be done by the addition of milk of lime gradually to the influent or by adding lime in the scum chamber. Care should be taken to prevent the addition of a large quantity of lime over a very short period of time as such sudden shocks of lime tend to upset digestion.

Imhoff Tank Operation: There are no mechanical parts in an Imhoff tank. Attention should, however, be given to the following:

1. Daily removal of grease, scum, and floating solids from the sedimentation compartment.

2. Weekly scraping of the sides and sloping bottoms of the sedimentation compartment by a rubber squeegee to remove adhering solids which may decompose.

3. Weekly cleaning the slot at the bottom of the sedimentation compartment. This can be done by use of a chain drag.

4. At least monthly reversal of flow where this is provided for in the design of the tank.

5. Control of the scum in the scum chamber by breaking it up, hosing with water under pressure, keeping it wet with sewage from the sedimentation compartment and removal if the depth approaches two to three feet.

6. Removal of sludge should be done before the sludge depth approaches within 18 inches of the slot in the sedimentation compartment. It is better to remove small amounts frequently than large amounts at long intervals. Sludge should be removed at a slow regular rate to avoid the formation of a channel through the sludge which would permit partially digested sludge and liquid held in storage above the digested sludge to be withdrawn from the tank. Before winter temperatures are expected, most of the digested sludge except that necessary for seeding (about 20 percent) should be removed to provide space for winter accumulations when digestion is very slow. The height of the sludge in the sludge compartment should be determine at inlet and outlet ends of the tank at least once a month. The use of a pump for this purpose is the most desirable and satisfactory. The use of the plate or disc method is not usually satisfactory. The following are suitable methods for measuring the depth of sludge:

    a. One method involves the use of a pitcher pump provided with a rubber suction hose, weighted on the end and the length marked on the hose at intervals of two feet, measuring from the weighted end toward the pump. The hose is gradually lowered through the slot in the sedimentation compartment, meanwhile constantly pumping, and the length of immersed hose, when sludge first comes through the pump is determined. When the sludge elevation is reached, the pump will usually "choke" before sludge appears.

27

b. A pitcher pump may also be used with a rubber suction hose, weighted on the end by a four foot length of steel pipe as an integral part of the pump suction line. This suction hose may be graduated and marked as above and the determination of sludge depth made in the same manner except that the hose is lowered through the gas vent instead of the sedimentation compartment slot.

c. The sludge depth may also be determined by use of an iron plate or weighted wooden block, about 12-18 inches square, attached to a wire or chain lowered through the gas vent. The plate or block will stop when the sludge is reached and the distance from the surface to the sludge level is determined from the graduated wire or chain by which the device is lowered.

d. Where the condition of gas vents will permit the use of a lighter implement, a modification of the above may be used. This consists of a wire loop, 12 or 15 inches in diameter, covered with a disc of a quarter inch mesh wire. A very light chain should be used with this disc suspended at three points.

7. After each time that sludge is removed, the sludge pipes should be flushed and filled with water or sewage to prevent sludge from hardening in and clogging the pipes.

8. Prevention of "Foaming": Every effort should be made to prevent "foaming" because correction after the condition arises is sometimes difficult. "Foaming" is usually associated with an acid condition of the sludge and in such cases may be prevented or corrected by treatment with lime to counteract the acidity of the sludge. When foaming occurs, it is usually desirable to seek the advice of an expert sanitary engineer. There are, however, a few simple measures which may under certain circumstances remedy or improve the condition.

   a. The use of hydrated lime added to the gas vents of Imhoff tanks or to the sludge added to separate digesters will usually aid in correction. The pH value of the resulting sludge and lime mixture in the digestion compartment should not exceed 7.6.

   b. Removing the tank from service where possible for a few days and allowing it to rest will sometimes improve conditions.

   c. In case of Imhoff tanks, agitation of the gas vent area with a water hose or paddles will sometimes help.

   d. When foaming occurs in separate digestion tanks, the gas line should be shut off or disconnected until the tank becomes normal again in order to protect the gas lines and gas control equipment from the foam solids.

   e. Lowering the temperature of the sludge in separate digesters for several days will reduce the foaming activity.

FIGURE 7
IMHOFF TANK – USEFUL EQUIPMENT

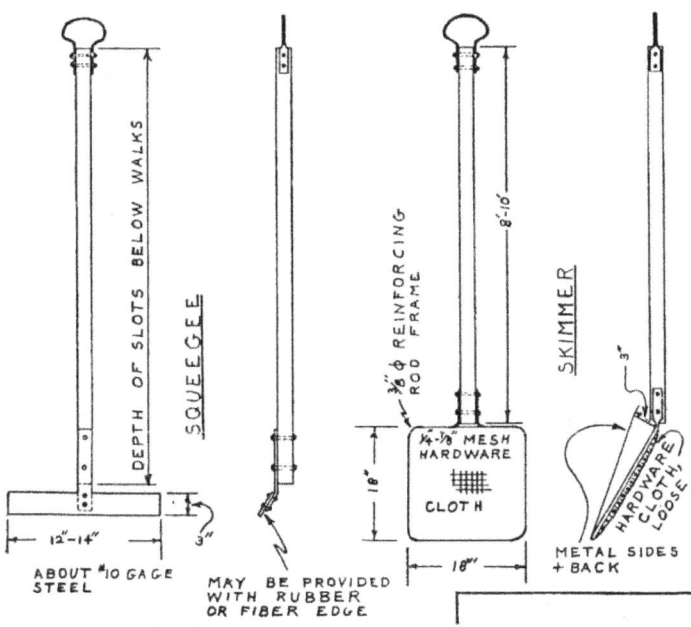

The Imhoff tank has no mechanical problems and is relatively easy and economical to operate. It provides sedimentation and sludge digestion in one unit and should produce a satisfactory primary effluent with a suspended solids removal of 40 to 60 percent and a BOD reduction of 25 to 35 percent. The two-story design requires a deep overall tank. Other more recently developed types of tanks have largely replaced the Imhoff tank for large municipal installations. The Imhoff tank is best suited to small municipalities and large institutions where the tributary population is 5,000 or less.

Operators interested in operation and maintenance of Imhoff tanks will find an excellent article by L.W. VanKleeck in the February 1956 issue4 of *Wastes Engineering*, entitled, "Operation of Imhoff Tanks."

Other Two-story Tanks: A number of manufacturers have put on the market prefabricated parts to be installed in tanks constructed according to their designs to produce two-story tanks embodying the Imhoff tank principle. These are patented units with trade names and are classed as "package units".

They provide separate compartments for sedimentation and sludge digestion in one tank. Facilities for heating the digestion compartment can be installed, if desired. The units are circular in shape and made in sizes to serve populations up to 5,000.

Provision is made for the collection and utilization of digestion gas and there are special features such as radial, tangential, and upward flow of the sewage. Some units have mechanical equipment for moving settled solids and sludge to outlets over relatively flat

29

surfaces. This permits reduction in depth of the sedimentation and digestion compartments and lowers the cost of tank construction.

PLAIN SEDIMENTATION TANKS

These are tanks whose major function is to remove settleable solids from the sewage b the process of sedimentation. The settled solids are taken from the tanks continuously or at frequent intervals so that decomposition with gas formation does not have time to develop. The solids are then handled by other units. The solids may flow by gravity to a hopper or to a low point in the bottom of the tank from which they are pumped or removed by hydrostatic pressure. This method, however, has been replaced by the use of mechanical equipment for the collection of the solids in a hopper from which they are removed by pumps. Tanks with mechanical equipment for the collection of solids are known as mechanically cleaned plain sedimentation tanks.

Mechanically Cleaned Plain Sedimentation Tanks: These tanks may be rectangular, circular, or square, but all operate on the same principle of collecting the settled solids by slow moving scrapers to the point of removal.

In the rectangular tanks the scrapers are attached near their ends to two endless chains which pass over sprockets driven by motors. The scrapers are dragged slowly along the tank floor pushing the settled solids to a sludge hopper located at the inlet end of the tank. The scrapers are then lifted by the chains to the surface of the tank where, partially submerged, they serve to push floating solids, grease, and oil to a scum collector at the outlet end of the tank. Another type of mechanism consists of a traveling bridge spanning the tank from which is suspended a blade to push solids to the point of removal and a skimmer blade for floating solids, grease, and oil. These blades operate when traveling in one direction and idle when traveling in the return direction.

FIGURE 8
RECTANGULAR-PLAIN SEDIMENTATION TANK

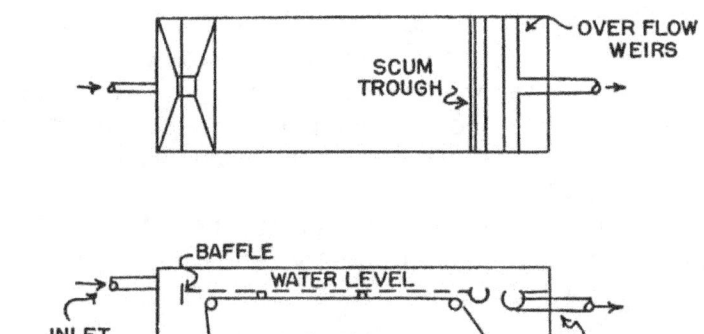

FIGURE 9
CIRCULAR-PLAIN SEDIMENTATION TANK

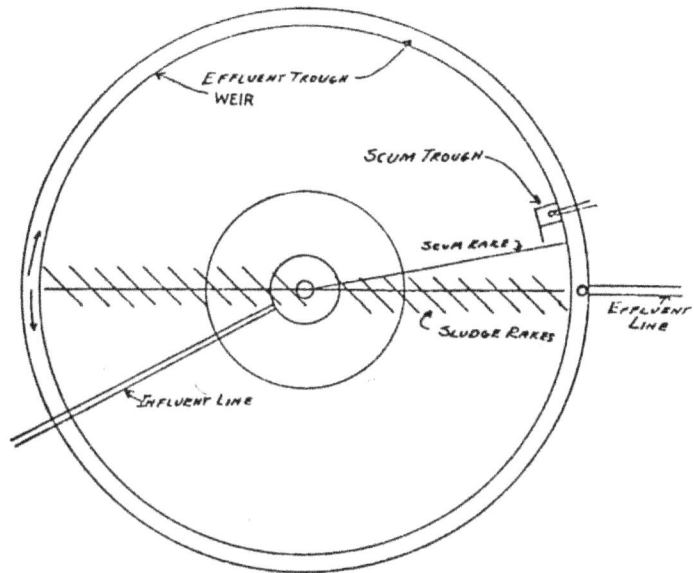

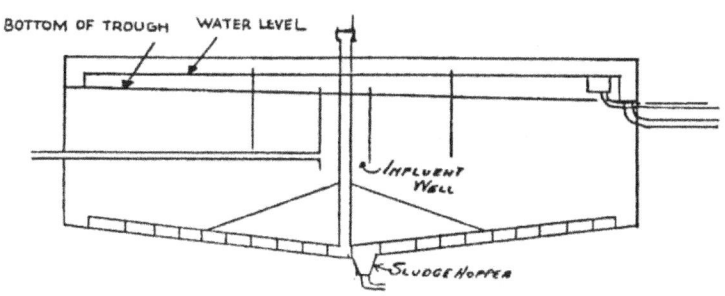

The circular tanks have scrapper arms attached to a central motor-driven shaft. The bottom of the tanks are sloped toward the center and the scrappers move the settled solids to a sludge hopper at the center. Skimmer arms are attached to the central shaft at the surface for the collection of floating solids, greases, and oil.

In the square tanks the mechanism is similar to that in the circular tanks. The major difference is that one or both of the rigid arms of the mechanism are equipped with pivoted corner blades which reach out into the four corners of the tank and move the solids in these areas to the path of the circular mechanism.

In the rectangular tanks the sewer enters at one end and flows horizontally to the other end. In the circular tanks sewage enters at the center and flows radially and generally horizontally to the periphery. In the square tanks the sewage may enter at the center and flow to the four sides or at one side and flow across the tank.

Several manufacturers have designed equipment to carry the incoming sewage close to the bottom of the tank from which it flows upward and radially through a sludge blanket to the outlet on the periphery. These are known as upward flow clarifiers and have the value of introducing the solids at the bottom where they are wanted instead of settling them from the upper layers.

FIGURE 10
PRIMARY TREATMENT

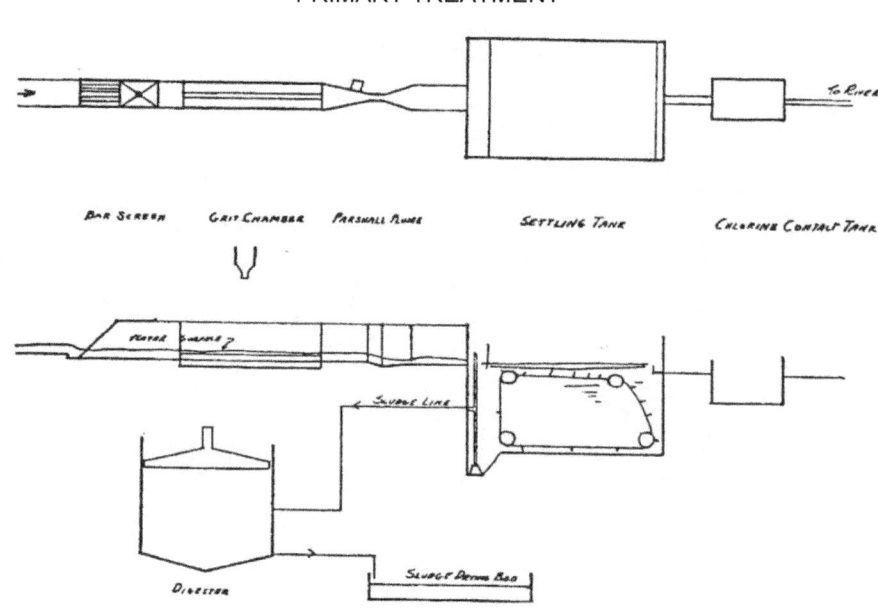

Manufacturers of mechanical equipment have given trade names to tanks using equipment manufactured by them. This Manual cannot detail the different equipment or comment on the claims made by the manufacturers for their specific designs. There are, however, general features common to all primary settling tanks. New York State has adopted the standards of the Upper Mississippi River Board of Public Health Engineers and Great Lakes Board of Public Health Engineers which are commonly referred to as the Ten States Standards.

Inlets: Inlets should be designed to dissipate the inlet velocity, diffuse the flow equally across the entire cross-section of the tank and prevent short-circuiting. They may be of the weir type but are more commonly a channel with spaced port openings.

Baffles: These are usually found at the inlet and outlet of a tank, the former to assist in diffusing the flow and the latter to hold back floating material from the tank effluent. Mechanically cleaned tanks usually have a scum trough which serves the purpose of the outlet baffle and to which scum is brought by the skimmer. Scum baffles should be provided ahead of outlet weirs on all primary settling tanks, on all final settling tanks in plants not having primary settling facilities and on all non-mechanical final settling tanks.

Outlet Weirs: These vary greatly in design. They are for the purpose of removing the settled sewage as a thin sheet from the surface of the tank and are usually adjustable. It is important that they be kept level for uniform surface removal. The term "*weir loading*" is used to express the gallons per day passing over one foot of the weir. In plants of one mgd or less capacity, this should not exceed 10,000 gallons per linear foot per day, which may be increased to 15,000 for larger plants.

Surface Settling Rate: This is expressed in terms of gallons per square foot of tank area based on the sewage flow per day. For primary tanks not followed by secondary treatment, this rate should not exceed 600 gallons per square foot per day for plants of one mgd or less capacity but may be higher for larger plants. This rate is an important factor and appears to affect directly the percent removal of settleable solids and BOD.

Detention Period: This is the time in hours any sewage is held in the tank based on the sewage flow and tank volume, assuming total displacement and uniform flow through the settling compartment. This was at one time the commonly used factor of design. It has, however, been largely replaced by weir loading and surface settling rate. Based on design flow, detention periods should be at least 2.0 hours.

Overall Dimensions: Recent accepted standards are a minimum of 10.0 feet in length and a liquid depth (mechanically cleaned) of not less than 7.0 feet. The amount of sewage to be treated, the general layout of the sewage treatment plant, the surface settling rate, and manufacturer's equipment determine the tank dimensions. Recent studies have indicated advantages in not making tanks too deep.

The following examples illustrate the use of the foregoing factors to evaluate the operating features of a sedimentation tank. Assume that one million gallons per day is being treated in a rectangular tank 70 feet long, 24 feet wide, and 7 feet deep. The outlet weirs are "H" shaped with four approaches 24 feet long, and two approaches 2 feet long.

Weir Loading
   $4 \times 24 + 2 \times 2 = 100$ ft. total weir length

   $$\frac{1{,}000{,}000 \text{ gal.}}{100 \text{ ft.}} = 10{,}000 \text{ gal./ft.}$$

Surface Settling Rate
   $24 \times 70 = 1{,}680$ sq. ft. surface area

   $$\frac{1{,}000{,}000 \text{ gal.}}{1{,}680 \text{ sq. ft.}} = 595, \text{ gal./sq. ft./day}$$

Detention Period
   $1{,}680 \times 7 \times 7.5 = 88{,}200$ gal. tank volume

   $$\frac{88{,}200 \times 24 \text{ gal.}}{000{,}000 \text{ ft.}} = 2.12, \text{ or about two hours detention}$$

Efficiency of Plain Sedimentation Tanks: Since the process of settling solids in plain sedimentation tanks is the same as in the sedimentation compartment of two-story tanks, similar results may be expected in their operation. About 90 to 95 percent of the settleable solids, and 40 to 60 percent of the total suspended solids, should be removed from the sewage. The BOD should be reduced by about 25 to 35 percent. Such figures are, of course, general and may not apply to specific cases. Sewage with high suspended solids may have a higher percentage removed by sedimentation than sewage with a low suspended solids content, but the suspended solids in the tank effluent may still be greater in the former. A higher percent removal can be expected in a tank treating fresh sewage than in one treating the same sewage after it has become septic because the solids in the septic sewage have been broken up or disintegrated by bacterial decomposition during their long travel in the sewer system. The amount and composition of industrial wastes are also an important factor affecting the percentage removal of suspended solids and BOD by primary settling tanks.

Operation of Mechanically Cleaned Sedimentation Tanks: The establishment and maintenance of proper time schedules for operation of the mechanical cleaning equipment and for removal of sludge from the tank are most important factors in tank operation. They must be determined for each plant. At most plants the collecting mechanisms are run from two to eight hours a day, depending on the size of the plant and the quantity of sludge produced. Very often circular tank mechanisms are run continuously. They should be run often enough to prevent a build-up of solids on the tank bottom. If the solids are allowed to build up in the tank, an undue load may be placed on the mechanism and cause damage to the equ9ipment. Solids may also be decomposed with the resultant production of gas in the settling tank and some floating sludge. Before sludge is removed from the tank, the mechanism should be run for a sufficient time to assure satisfactory collection of bottom solids in the sludge hopper.

Sludge should be removed from the tank at least daily. It is not good practice to remove sludge with an excessive amount of water as this water wastes storage space and heat in digestion tanks. Maintaining a sludge blanket of 12 to 18 inches in the sludge hopper and pumping small amounts at frequent intervals and at a low rate helps to obtain sludge of a higher solids concentration. The sludge pump should have a sampling tap. As a guide, if a sample of sludge in a test jar after setting for ten minutes shows more than a 50 percent volume of sludge, pumping should be continued. If it shows less than 50 percent, removal may be considered reasonably complete. A vacuum gauge on the suction side of the pump and a pressure gauge on the discharge line are valuable. Should either gauge show zero, the operator will know that the line is plugged. A decreasing reading on the pressure gauge shows that the sludge is getting thinner. The sludge removal schedule must be worked out for each plant by observation and tests, keeping in mind that the objective is not to see how fast sludge can be removed but to remove a concentrated sludge while it is still fresh and to have the floor of the tank clean after a removal cycle. Seasonal revision of the schedule will probably be necessary.

Scum and grease should be removed daily from the surface of the tank. Most mechanical collectors direct such material to a grease trough from which it flows to a grease well for disposal by pumping to the digestion tank or by other means.

Where there is more than one tank, poor flow distribution often accounts for poor operation. The operator should check his particular installation to be sure that each tank is receiving its share of the load. When it is found that one tank is receiving more or less than its share, the inlet arrangements should be checked to ascertain whether a manipulation can be made to equalize the flow to each tank. The elevation of all effluent weirs should be checked as uneven weirs can do a great deal to increase short circuiting and unequal flow distribution. When it is necessary to pump to a sedimentation tank, the flow should be at as even a rate as possible to obtain the best possible results.

At all times the operator must be conscious that mechanical equipment requires attention and maintenance. Moving parts must be kept lubricated and weak or worn parts replaced. The best rule is to rigidly follow the instruction manual provided by the manufacturer of the equipment.

Advantages and Disadvantages of Mechanically Cleaned Plain Sedimentation Tanks with Separate Sludge Digestion: Except for relatively small installations, this type of tank has almost universal use in this country and it is being used more and more in the smaller municipal and larger institutional plants.

There are two main reasons for this: (1) the treatment of sludge in separate tanks, especially heated tanks, provides more complete control of the digestion process, and (2) the cost of construction especially for large units is less.

These tanks do, however, require more time and competency in operation than the Imhoff tank, because of the operational requirement and the care and maintenance of mechanical equipment.

CHEMICAL TREATMENT

Chemical treatment has been conventionally classed as intermediate treatment, in that the results obtained by it are greater than with standard primary treatment but less than with secondary treatment. It is included in this Manual under primary treatment because it involves chemical and physical processes as distinct from the biological processes which are the basis of secondary treatment.

Chemical treatment is one of the older methods of sewage treatment which fell into discard but was reintroduced in the decade 1930-40. However, developments in secondary treatment methods, the supervision needed, the cost of chemicals, and the excessive amounts of sludge requiring disposal have caused this method of treatment to be restricted to special conditions. It still has application in the treatment of industrial wastes which are not easily attacked biologically and where conditions in the receiving waters periodically require a higher degree of treatment than standard primary treatment, but do not warrant secondary treatment.

Chemical treatment involves the addition of one or more chemicals to sewage to produce a floc which is an insoluble chemical compound that absorbs colloidal matter, enmeshes non-settleable suspended solids and settles readily. The precipitating chemical also dissociates or ionizes in the sewage and neutralizes the electric charges held by colloidal particles causing them to coalesce to form larger readily settleable solids. The chemicals most widely used are aluminum sulfate or alum, ferrous sulfate with lime, ferric sulfate and ferric chloride with or without lime.

A chemical treatment plant usually has the following features:

1. Preliminary devices—screens, grit chambers, etc. as described in Chapter 4
2. Chemical feeders
3. Mixing units
4. Flocculation tanks
5. Sedimentation tanks such as have already been described
6. Increased facilities for the treatment and disposal of sludge

Chemical Feeders: A large variety of units to feed chemicals, either dry or in solution, in controlled amounts are made by a number of manufacturers. Details are not warranted in this Manual.

Mixing Units: The chemicals when added to sewage must be thoroughly and quickly mixed with it to provide complete and uniform reactions. This is accomplished by violent agitation for a short period of time either by mechanical or hydraulic methods. This agitation is carried on in special tanks, in sections of other tanks, or in the piping system. Mixing devices are made by a number of manufacturers.

Flocculators: After the chemical is mixed with sewage, it is gently agitated for 15 to 30 minutes to foster the coagulation of particles. If BOD reduction is desired, the agitation time may be increased to 45 minutes. The colloidal and suspended solids meet and adhere together in large flocculant masses which settle readily in the sedimentation tank. Different types of equipment to accomplish this purpose are made by a number of manufacturers.

Sludge: The volume of sludge obtained by chemical treatment is greater than with standard primary treatment, necessitating a comparable increase in sludge handling facilities and cost of sludge treatment and disposal.

Efficiency: Chemical treatment can effect a reduction up to 90 percent in suspended solids and up to 70 percent in the BOD. It is well adapted to intermittent operation and has value in sewage treatment to reduce pollution of streams during periods of low flow or to lessen pollution of bathing beaches and recreational waters during months when these facilities are in use. It is of value also for the treatment of sewage containing high concentrations of industrial wastes which will inhibit biological life and interfere with secondary treatment processes.

35

Operation costs are high due to increase in operators' time, chemicals, and greater quantities of sludge to be treated and disposed of.

Operation: Because of its limited use in sewage treatment operation, details regarding the usage of chemicals in chemical precipitation are not included in this Manual.

CHAPTER 6

SECONDARY TREATMENT

In many situations, primary treatment with the resulting removal of 40 to 60 percent of the suspended solids and approximately 25 to 35 percent of the BOD, together with the removal of floating material from the sewage, is adequate to meet requirements of the receiving water. However, if the accomplishment of primary treatment is not sufficient, there are two basic methods of secondary treatment available, trickling filters and activated sludge. Sand filters can be used when a high degree of treatment or a polishing effect is required. There are several other methods which are used to a limited extent. These types of treatment employ biological growths to effect aerobic decomposition or oxidation of organic material into more stable compounds and provide for a higher degree of treatment that accomplished by primary sedimentation alone.

While trickling filters and activated sludge both depend on aerobic biological organisms to effect decomposition, there is an operational difference. In filters the organisms are attached to the filter medium and the organic material on which they do their work is brought to them. With activated sludge, however, the organisms are migrant and are carried to the organic matter in the sewage. In either case, successful operation involves the maintenance of aerobic environmental conditions favorable for the life cycle of the organisms, and control over the amount of organic matter which they decompose. The organic matter is the food upon which these organisms live. If they are either over-fed or under-fed, their efficiency is reduced.

TRICKLING FILTERS

The word "filter" in this case is not correctly used, for there is no straining of filtering action involved. Actually, a trickling filter is a device for bring settled sewage into contact with biological growths. A more applicable name would be "biological oxidizing bed," but time and usage have made the term trickling filter a popular one and it is used universally to describe this type of unit.

Trickling filters are sturdy work units, not easily upset by shock loads, noted for their consistent performance, and capable of taking considerable abuse. Like all biological units they are affected by temperature; therefore, cold weather slows down biological activity in the filter. They occupy large areas and are expensive to construct.

For economy the filters should be preceded by primary sedimentation tanks equipped with scum collecting devices. Primary treatment ahead of filters makes available the full capacity of the filters for use in the conversion of non-settleable, colloidal, and dissolved solids, to readily settleable solids. These solids which are largely organic, are not removed from the sewage but are converted to living microscopic organisms or stable organic matter temporarily attached to the filter medium and to inorganic matter carried off with the effluent. The attached material eventually sloughs off and is carried away in the filter effluent. For this reason, trickling filters should be followed by secondary sedimentation tanks to remove permanently the solids from the sewage.

Construction: A typical trickling filter consists of three parts: (a) the bed of filter medium, (2) an underdrainage system, and (c) mechanism for distribution the sewage evenly over the surface of the filter.

1. The choice of filter media is often governed by the material locally available or the cost of bring material in. Field stone, gravel, broken stone, blast furnace slag, and anthracite coal have been used for this purpose. Redwood blocks and inert materials molded into appropriate shapes have also been employed. Whatever material is chosen, it is usually specified that it be sound, hard, clean, and free of dust and insoluble in sewage constituents. The material should be approximately cubical in shape to prevent compacting, and of a size to pass a four and one-half inch square screen, but be retained by a two inch square screen. The filter media should have a minimum depth of five feet and should not exceed seven feet in depth. The bed may be rectangular to circular. The former is common where distribution of sewage is by fixed spray nozzles, and the latter where rotating distributors are used as described under (3) below. The filter medium serves the dual purpose of providing a large surface area on which the slimes and gelatinous films produced by bacteria can develop yet leaving sufficient voids to permit free circulation of air throughout the filter.

2. *Underdrain System*: The underdrains serve two purposes: (1) to carry the sewage passing through the filter away from it for subsequent treatment and disposal, an (2) to provide for ventilation of the filter and the maintenance of aerobic condition. The direction of air flow through the filter depends on the difference in temperature between the filter and the sewage being applied. When the filter stone is warmer than the sewage, the direction of air will generally be upwards through the filter. When the temperature of the filter is colder, the direction of the air will be downward. The underdrain system consisting of precast filter blocks which are manufactured from vitrified clay or concrete, covers the entire bottom of the filter and leads to effluent channels. The blocks are usually rectangular in shape and have openings in the upper face equal to at least 20 percent of the surface of the block.

3. *Distributors*: Sewage is applied to the surface of the bed by fixed spray nozzles or rotary distributors. The fixed spray nozzles were used when trickling filters were first developed. The nozzles are attached to pipes laid in the filter medium and are fed intermittently from a siphon controlled dosing tank. By this method sewage is applied to the filter for short periods of time. Between applications, the filter has rest periods while the dosing tank is filling. Many types and shapes of nozzles have been developed and the siphon dosing tank is designed to attain the best possible even distribution of sewage over the entire surface of the filter. At best, the distribution is not even and there are areas of the filter on which very little sewage is sprayed.

Figure 11 shows diagrammatically a siphon controlled dosing tank. When the dosing tank has finished discharging, the level of the sewage is at the lower bend of the vent pipe. The sewage now stands at the level B_1 in both legs of the main trap. The blowoff trap is filled with sewage up to D_1 and the vent pipe is empty. As sewage rises in the dosing tank, it seals the open end of the vent pipe at "A" and prevents the escape of air from the bell. As the sewage continues to rise, the liquid level in the bell also rises. The air in the long leg of the main trap and of the blowoff trap is compressed and the surfaces of the sewage in these two legs are forced downward. When the dosing tank is filled to a point just below the discharge level, the surfaces of the sewage in the main trap and in the blowoff trap are at B_2 and D_2. A further rise of sewage level in the dosing tank causes the air in the bell to escape through the blowoff trap. The release of air causes an inrush of sewage from the dosing tank into the bell and down through the main trap, resulting in the dosing apparatus going into full operation. The discharge continues until the surface of the sewage reaches the lower elbow of the vent pipe. At this point air enters the bell through the vent pipe and the siphonic action is broken. The main trap and the blowoff trap remain filled with sewage. The vent pipe is empty and the cycle of filling and discharge commences again. The air vent in the discharge pipe allows escape of the air forced out of the bell and traps. Twin dosing tanks are often so interlocked that one may be filling while the other is discharging. There are many variations in design of dosing tanks. Some use mechanical devices to replace the main trap shown here.

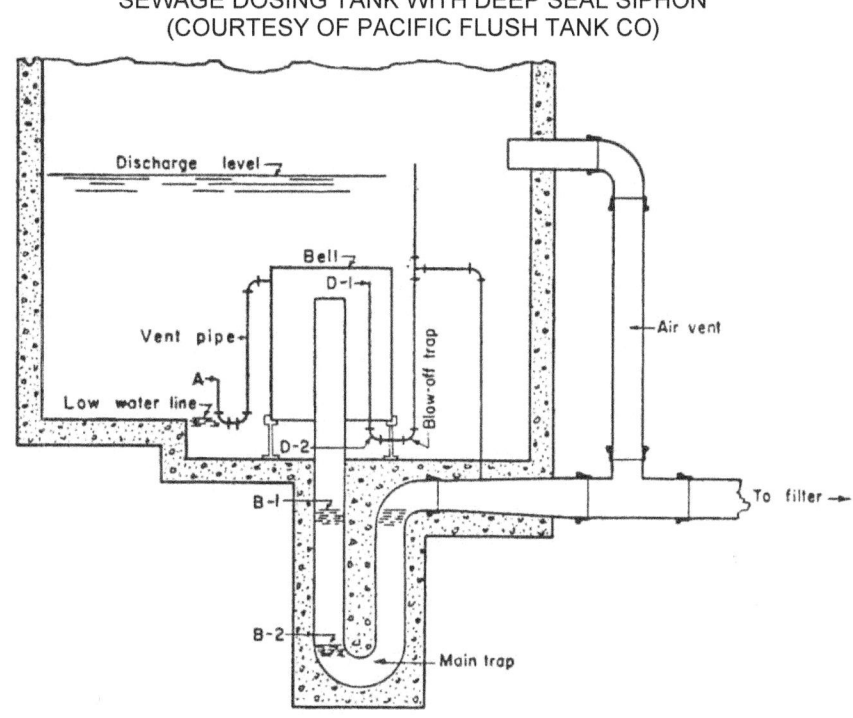

FIGURE 11
SEWAGE DOSING TANK WITH DEEP SEAL SIPHON
(COURTESY OF PACIFIC FLUSH TANK CO)

The fixed spray nozzles have been largely supplanted by rotary distributors which effect a more even dosage over the entire area of the bed. With the rotary distributors, sewage is fed through a hollow vertical center column to which are attached two or more arms. Each arm contains a number of nozzle openings, all of which point at right angles to the arms and through which sewage is applied to the surface of the filter. The central feed column and arms which revolve slowly over the surface of the circular filter are usually driven by jet action of the sewage as it discharges through the nozzles. Positive drive mechanisms also are available.

Loading: Filter loadings are commonly expressed in terms of hydraulic loading and organic load. The hydraulic load is the number of gallons of sewage applied per acre of filter surface per day, or more accurately, because of different depths of filters, per acre foot per day. The organic loading is the number of pounds of BOD per 1,000 cubic feet of filter medium. Pounds per acre foot or per cubic yard of filter medium also are used.

Based on hydraulic and BOD loadings, trickling filters are classified as "Standard" and "High Rate."

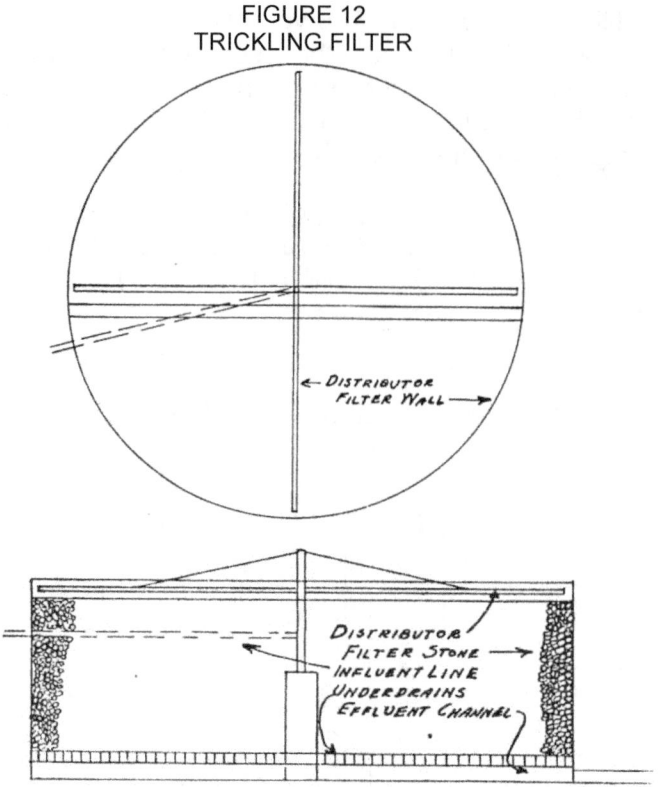

FIGURE 12
TRICKLING FILTER

Standard Trickling Filters: These are operated at a hydraulic loading of 1.1 to 4.4 million gallons per acre per day with an organic loading of 5.0 to 25.0 pounds per 1,000 cubic feet of filter medium per day. The following example illustrates how the loadings of an operating filter are obtained:

Suppose a filter 100 feet in diameter and six feet deep is receiving 0.5 mgd of primary tank effluent with a BOD of 150 ppm.

Area of filter (acres) = $\dfrac{\Pi d^2}{4 \times 43,560}$ = 0.18 acres

The hydraulic loading = $\dfrac{0.5}{.18}$ = 2.8 mgad (million gallons per acre per day)

The pounds of BOD applied = $0.5 \times 8.34 \times 150$ = 625 pounds per day.

The volume of filter medium $\dfrac{\Pi d^2}{4} \times 6$ = 47,124 cubic feet

The BOD loading = $\dfrac{625}{47,124} \times 1,000$ = 13.3 pounds of BOD per 1,000 cubic feet of filter medium per day

Sewage is applied intermittently with rest periods which generally do not exceed five minutes at the designed rate of sewage flow. With proper loadings, the standard trickling filter, including primary and secondary sedimentation units, should under normal operation remove from 80 to 85 percent of the applied BOD. While there is some unloading of solids at all times, which has accumulated on the filter medium, the major unloading occurs several times a year for comparatively short periods of time.

40

FIGURE 13
STANDARD RATE FILTER

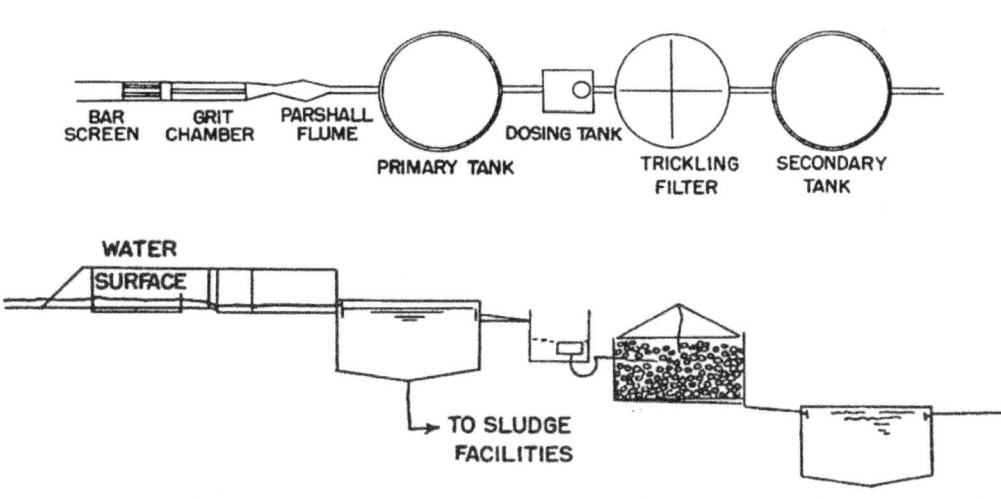

High Rate Trickling Filters: These units are operated with hydraulic loadings of 8.7 to 44.0 million gallons per acre per day and organic loadings of 25.0 to 50.0 pounds per cubic feet of filter medium per day.

When trickling filters were first developed, it was believed that their successful operation required rest periods between dosing. The application of sewage was, therefore, intermittent. It later developed that the rest periods between doses were not essential and had some detrimental effects. This enabled a major increase in the hydraulic loadings and some, though not a proportional, increase in the BOD loadings. The higher hydraulic rate was attained by mixing filter effluent with the normal sewage flow in proportions of up to ten to one and recirculating it through the filter. The higher BOD load is attained by applying a larger volume per acre of the normal sewage flow to the filter. This effects a reduction in the BOD concentration of the sewage as applied to the filter, even though the total BOD load per day is higher. The various ways by which this recirculation is accomplished are patented processes and are identified by trade names, some of which are as follows:

Biofilter: In the biofilter, a process is used involving recirculation and a high rate of application to a shallow trickling filter. The recirculation in this case involves brining the effluent of the filter or of the secondary sedimentation tank back through the primary settling tank. The secondary settling tank sludge is usually very light and can be continually fed back to the primary settling tank where the two types of sludges are collected together and pumped to the digester. See Figure 14a.

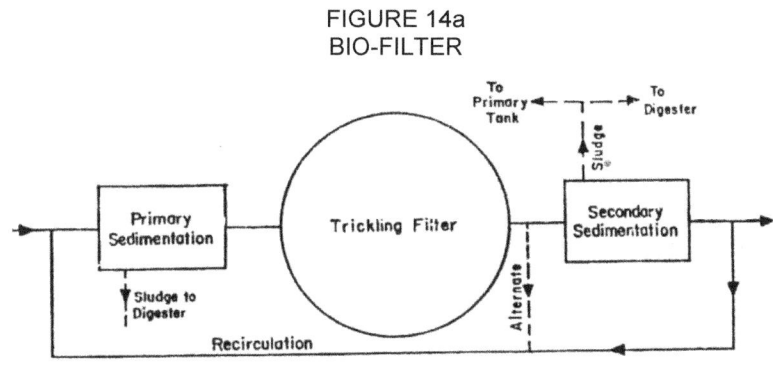

FIGURE 14a
BIO-FILTER

41

"Accelo" Filter: The accelo filter, another sewage treatment process, involves the recirculation of filter effluent directly back to the filter as shown in Figure 14b.

FIGURE 14b
ACCELO-FILTER

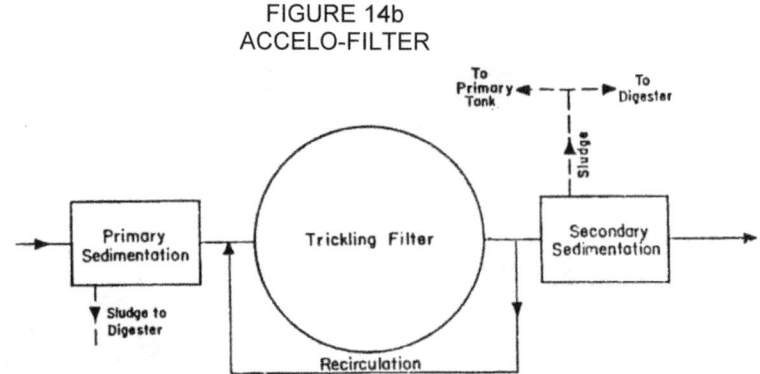

Aero-Filter: The aero-filter (Figure 14c) is still another process which distributes the sewage by maintaining a continuous rain-like application of the sewage over the filter bed. For small beds, distribution is accomplished by a disk distributor revolving at a high speed of 260 to 369 rpm set 20" above the surface of the filter to give a continuous rain-like distribution over the entire bed. For large beds, a large number of revolving distributor arms, 10 or more, tend to give more uniform distribution. These filters are always operated at a rate in excess of 10 million gallons per acre of surface per day.

FIGURE 14c
AERO-FILTER

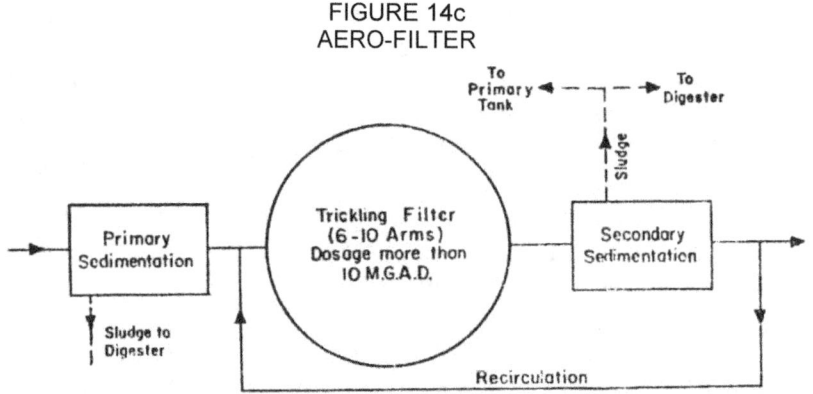

A typical combination for loadings of a high rate filter is as follows:

A filter 100 feet in diameter and six feet deep is receiving 1.0 mgd of normal settled sewage with a BOD of 150 ppm with recirculation at a rate of four to one or a total of 5 mg.

Area of filter (acres) = $\dfrac{\pi d^2}{4 \times 43,560}$ = 0.18 acres

Hydraulic loading = $\dfrac{5.0}{.18}$ = 27.7 mgad (million gallons per acre per day)

Pounds of BOD applied = 1 × 8.34 × 150 = 1,250 pounds per day.

Volume of filter medium = $\dfrac{\pi d^2}{4}$ × 6 = 47,124 cubic feet

BOD loading = $\dfrac{1,250}{625}$ × 1,000 = 26.6 pounds of BOD per 1,000 cubic feet of filter medium per day

42

High rate trickling filters, including primary and secondary sedimentation, should, under normal operation, remove from 65 to 80 percent of the BOD of the sewage. Recirculation should be adequate to provide continuous dosage at a rate equal to or in excess of 10 million gallons per acre per day with rest periods not more than 15 seconds. As a result of continuous dosing at such high rates, some of the solids accumulated on the filter medium are washed off and carried away with the effluent continuously, and there are no intermittent unloading periods.

High rate trickling filters have been used advantageously for pre-treatment of industrial wastes and unusually strong sewage. When so used, they are called *"roughing filters."* With these, the BOD loading is usually in excess of 110 pounds of BOD per 1,000 cubic feet of filter medium.

Two high rate filters in series have been used to effect a higher degree of treatment and produce a final settled effluent of less than 30 ppm of BOD.

The following table contains comparative data on a number of features of standard and high rate trickling filters.

TABLE 1

	Hydraulic Loading Mil. Gal. Per Acre Per Day	BOD Loading Pounds BOD per 1,000 Cu. Ft. Filter Medium	Operation	Unloading	Percent BOD Removal Including Primary and Secondary Sedimentation
Standard	1-4	Less than 15	Intermittent	Largely Periodic	80-85
High Rate	10-30	30-110	Continuous	Continuous	65-80

Operation: As both standard and high rate trickling filters are biological workshops, the principles of operation are the same, and the troubles encountered with their maintenance are similar.

The nozzles, whether fixed spray or on rotators, should be inspected daily and all those found clogged or damaged should be cleaned or repaired.

During winter months careful attention is required to prevent freezing, especially with standard rate filters where intermittent operation causes periods of quiescence which are more conducive to freezing than with the continuous operation and constant motion of liquid in high rate filters. There is a tendency of some operators to by-pass the filters during the winter months. This practice should not be a general procedure. A trickling filter should be continued in operation except for brief periods when ice formation is sufficient to cause damage to the distribution system.

The distribution system, whether fixed or moving, should be flushed periodically, preferably daily, to remove any material which might cause clogging. If possible, the underdrains also should be hosed out occasionally.

Where the distribution system involves mechanical equipment with moving parts, the only safe rule is to know well and follow rigidly the instructions in the service manual which the manufacturer supplies for his particular equipment. It should be used, not filed or lost.

The surface of the filter must be kept free from weed growths and accumulation of leaves or other debris. Trees or shrubs in close proximity to a filter should be removed.

A number of chemicals may be received by a sewer system, generally in industrial wastes, which in appreciable concentration are toxic or poisonous to biological life. When the normal efficiency of a filter shows a somewhat sudden drop, immediate checks should be made at industrial plants tributary to the sewer system to determine if there has been a discharge of toxic material into the sewers and to arrange for its elimination or pre-treatment by the industry.

To provide uniform distribution of sewage over the bed practically all rotary distributors require periodic adjustment of the turnbuckles on the guy rods to the arms. This is needed in order to maintain the proper level of the arms and their distance from the surface of the filter. In hot weather the rods become longer and the turnbuckles should be taken up slightly to compensate for the metal expansion due to heat. In cold weather the condition is reversed and the turnbuckles should be let out.

Ponding of filters will occur if the voids in the filter medium become clogged and the free passage of liquid is prevented. This may be due to the use of too small filter medium or disintegrated filter medium. The only way to permanently correct this difficulty is to replace the filter medium with material of proper size and quality. It, however, the voids become filled by prolific growths of organisms and slimes on the surface of the filter medium, there are corrective measures available to the operation which should be employed as soon as ponding is evident. These measures include:

1. Flushing the surface of the ponded area with a fire hose.
2. Applying heavy doses of chlorine for short periods, either directly to the ponding area or to the sewage influent. The latter can best be done at night when the chlorine demand of the sewage is lowest. Chlorine doses up to 5 ppm will kill the excessive growth in the filter.
3. Flooding the entire filter and allowing it to stand full for 24 hours.
4. Cutting the filter out of service and allowing it to stand unused for several days.
5. Temporarily increasing the rate of recirculation. This can be done only where the filters are so designed to permit this method of operation.

Ponding is always an indication that something is wrong, and indicates to the operator not only to use the corrective measures outlined above, but to check the operation of the entire treatment plant for possible cause. If primary units are not properly removing grease or oils, the biological film on the filter medium will be coated, and the organisms will be deprived of oxygen and the sewage kept from contact with the organisms. It may be that the filter installation is inadequate for the plant load. This, of course, calls for the installation of additional units which should be constructed as soon as possible.

Another troublesome condition which frequently develops at trickling filter installations is the excessive production of the filter fly—the psychoda. These flies are so small that they can pass through an ordinary window screen and are very bothersome to the plant operator and nearby neighbors.

The larvae of the flies prefer a breeding place which is damp but not too wet and are, therefore, more prevalent in standard rate filters with intermittent dosages than in high rate filters with continuous dosing. Some of these insects may be present in a normal filter unit which is functioning properly, as the filter fly is one of the natural biological organisms which feeds on the sludge and film growth and assists in the decomposition of organic matter. However, excessive numbers indicate that the biological life in the filter is unbalanced, probably due to organic overloading.

The control of filter flies has proven to be very difficult. Keeping all parts of the filter wet, especially the edges, will discourage their breeding. Numerous insecticides such as D.D.T., chordane, lindane, and others have been tried to rid an infested filter of these pests. None have been completely satisfactory except to give temporary relief. The use of any one insecticide seems to result in the development of resistant strains of the insect. It has been found that it is better to use several in rotation. This treatment is expensive and extreme caution is necessary as too heavy a dose may kill all the desirable and necessary biological life in the filter.

If duplicate filter units are available, one can be taken out of service for a day or two and either flooded or allowed to dry out to create conditions in the filter unfavorable for the fly development.

Although any one of the above may give temporary relief, the only permanent solution to the psychoda nuisance is, as in ponding control, to determine its cause and then to provide corrective action.

Since the operation of the trickling filter depends on biological life, it is evident that when one is first put into service it takes time to build up an adequate population of organisms on the filter medium. This is true not only of a new unit but also of one which has been idle long enough to have the organisms die for want of food and water. Bypassing a unit for any prolonged period should, if possible, be avoided.

Every trickling filter installation has its own particular characteristics. There appears to be no one method of operation best suited to all plants. Advantage should be taken of any provisions for flexible operation which are available, and different methods of operation such as parallel or series flow should be tried to determine the best conditions for the particular plant.

SECONDARY SEDIMENTATION TANKS

Since trickling filters merely alter the character but do not remove solids from the sewage, the effluent contains suspended solids which should be removed before disposal by discharge to receiving waters.

For this purpose, secondary sedimentation tanks or final settling tanks are used. These tanks are similar in design to those described in Chapter 5 on Primary Treatment and should provide a surface settling rate not in excess of 800 gallons per square foot per day based on design flow.

ACTIVATED SLUDGE

The development of the activated sludge process marked an important advance in the secondary treatment of sewage. Like the trickling filter, it is a biological contact process where living aerobic organisms and the organic solids in the sewage are brought together in an environment favorable for the aerobic decomposition of the solids. Since the environment is the sewage itself, efficient operation of the process is dependent on the continual maintenance of dissolved oxygen at all times throughout the sewage being treated. The environment itself, however, accomplishes little unless it is inhabited by enough living workers.

Normal sewage contains some of these biological workers but the number is far too small to do the work at hand. It is necessary, therefore, to add many more organisms and to distribute them throughout the sewage before the activated sludge process can begin to function with any efficiency.

The activated sludge process is usually employed following plain sedimentation. The sewage contains some suspended and colloidal solids and, when agitated in the presence of air, the suspended solids form nuclei on which biological life develop and gradually build up to larger solids which are known as activated sludge.

Activated sludge is a brownish floc-like substance consisting largely of organic matter obtained from the sewage, and inhabited b myriads of bacteria and other forms of biological life. Activated sludge with its living organisms has the property of absorbing or adsorbing colloidal and dissolved organic matter including ammonia from sewage so that the suspended solids are reduced. The biologic organisms utilize the absorbed material as food and convert it into insoluble non-putrescible solids. Much of this conversion is a step-by-step process. Some bacteria attack the original complex substances to produce simpler compounds as their waste products. Other bacteria use these waste products to produce still simpler compounds and the process continues until the final waste products can no longer be used as food for bacteria.

The generation of activated sludge or floc in sewage is a slow process, and the amount so formed from any volume of sewage during its period of treatment is small and inadequate for the rapid and effective treatment of the sewage which requires large concentrations of activated sludge. Such concentration is built up by collecting the sludge produced from each volume of sewage treated and re-using it in the treatment of subsequent sewage flows. The sludge so re-used is known as *return sludge*. This is a cumulative process so that eventually more sludge has been produced and is available for re-use than is needed. The surplus or *excess activated sludge*, is then permanently removed from the treatment process and conditioned for ultimate disposal.

The activated sludge must be kept in suspension during its period of contact with the sewage being treated by some method of agitation. This activated sludge process, therefore, consists of the following steps:

1. Mixing the activated sludge with the sewage to be treated.
2. Aeration and agitation of this mixed liquor for the required length of time.
3. Separation of the activated sludge from the mixed liquor.
4. Return of the proper amount of activated sludge for mixture with the sewage.
5. Disposal of the excess activated sludge.

A number of variations in carrying out the steps given above have been developed to meet different conditions. This has resulted in using the term "conventional activated sludge" for the original activated sludge process and giving specific names to the variations of the original process.

Before considering these variations, it is desirable to define two terms which are commonly used, and to consider the basic steps involved in the activated sludge process.

Sludge Volume Index is the volume in ml of one gram of activated sludge in the mixed liquor which has settled for thirty minutes. The best sludge volume index must be determined for each plant and slight variations from day to day are to be expected, but a rising sludge volume index indicates that the volume occupied by one gram of sludge is increasing, causing a loss in density and a tendency towards bulking which is discussed later.

Sludge Age is the average time in days a particle of suspended solids remains under aeration in the activated sludge sewage treatment process. It is calculated from the weight of activated sludge in the aeration tank and the suspended solids in the sewage entering the aeration tank using the formula:

$$\text{Sludge age} = \frac{V \times A}{Q \times C}$$

V = volume of aeration tank in mg
A = concentration of suspended solids in the aeration tank in ppm
Q = sewage flow in mgd
C = concentration of suspended solids in the sewage entering the aeration tank in ppm exclusive of returned sludge

The sludge age must be kept within certain limits for satisfactory operation, depending on the character of the sewage being treated and must be determined for each plant. For an average domestic sewage a sludge age of three to four days is generally satisfactory.

Mixing the Activated Sludge With the Sewage to be Treated: It is very important that the returned activated sludge be thoroughly mixed with the sewage. This is generally accomplished by adding the return sludge to the settled sewage at the inlet end of the aeration tank in which the agitation provides rapid and satisfactory mixing. In some cases small mixing chambers with

46

agitation are provided, but this is not common practice.

Aeration and Agitation of Mixed Liquor: Aeration accomplishes three objects: mixing the returned activated sludge with the sewage, keeping the sludge in suspension by agitation of the mixture, and supplying the oxygen required for biological oxidation. Air is generally added by one of two methods known as "diffused air" or "pressure aeration" system or by mechanical aeration.

In the *diffused air system*, air under low pressure, generally not more than eight to ten pounds, is supplied by blowers and forced through various types of porous material in plates or tubes which break up the air into fine bubbles. These plates or tubes are so located in the aeration tank that a rotary motion is imparted to the sewage mixture resulting in a considerable amount of air being absorbed from the atmosphere. Diffuser plates are composed of fused crystalline alumina or a high-silica sand. They are set in containers usually made of reinforced concrete. Diffuser tubes are made of similar material or, more recently, of corrugated stainless steel pipe with multiple outlets and wrapped with saran twisted cord. These are suspended in the aeration tank in sections and can be disconnected above the sewage surface and removed for cleaning or renewal. When installed on swing joint connections so that they may be brought to the surface of the tank, they are known as "Swing Diffuser."

To prevent clogging of the diffuser plates or tubes, the air to them should be filtered to remove dust, oil, or other impurities, and the piping should be of non-corrosive material. There are a number of types of filters available based on different principles which may be used alone or in combination.

Mechanical Aerators ae of two general types—paddle and vertical draft tube. The paddle type consists of a paddle wheel or brush partly submerged in the sewage revolving on a horizontal axis. Air is absorbed by surface contact and by droplets thrown through the air by the paddle mechanism. With the vertical draft tube sewage is drawn up or down through a central vertical tube by a revolving impeller. There are a number of types of the vertical draft tube aerator made by different manufacturers, each with special patented features.

In addition to the above two methods, there are several other types of aerators on the market using different devices to introduce or entrain air and provide agitation.

Air Requirements are governed by:

1. The BOD loading
2. The quality of the activated sludge
3. The solids concentration
4. The desired efficiency in BOD removal

The basic air requirement is that there shall be sufficient air added to the sewage to maintain in it at least two ppm of dissolved oxygen under all conditions of loading in all parts of the aeration tanks except immediately beyond the inlets. Tests for dissolved oxygen should be made in different sections of the tank to assure that this value is maintained.

In the diffused air systems, the amount of air added is often stated in terms of the cubic feet of air per gallon of sewage, usually ranging from one-half to one and one-half. A preferable method of expression, now more commonly used, is in terms of cubic feet of air per pound of BOD to be removed from the primary tank effluent. Normal requirements are assumed to be 1,000 cu. ft. per pound of BOD, and the air system should be capable of delivering 150 percent of this figure.

The above figures apply generally to a normal domestic sewage in a conventional type activated sludge plant as defined later. Where industrial wastes are involved or the plant is one of the modified types (also defined later), major variation from these figures may occur and must be determined by operating experience at each plant. Insufficient air will result in a deterioration of the quality of the activated sludge and a serious breakdown of plant efficiency. The use of excessive amounts of air is not only wasteful but may result in a sludge so finely dispersed that it becomes difficult to settle.

Aeration Time: In the activated sludge process, the sludge accomplishes the major part of the removal of BOD and solids from the sewage being treated in a relatively short period of aeration. It takes, however, a much longer time for the sludge to assimilate the organic matter which it has absorbed. During this time an aerobic environment must be maintained. To effect the most complete treatment of sewage and most economical operation in the conventional activated sludge process, an aeration time of six to eight hours has been found to be adequate for diffused air aeration and nine to twelve hours for mechanical aeration. Materially shorter periods are used in some of the modifications of the conventional process. These shorter aeration periods generally result in a lowering of the quality of the plant effluents. This is described later under the various types of activated sludge plants.

Separation of Activated Sludge from the Mixed Liquor: Before the sewage treated in the aeration tank can be disposed of by discharging into receiving waters, the activated sludge must be removed. This is done in secondary or final settling tanks. These tanks are similar in design to the mechanically cleaned primary sedimentation tanks described in Chapter 5. Surface settling rates should not exceed 800 gallons per square foot per day.

The cycle of sludge removal from the secondary tanks is much more important than with primary tanks. Some sludge is being removed continuously to be used as returned sludge in the aeration tanks. The excess sludge must be removed before it loses its activity because of the death of the aerobic organism resulting from lack of oxygen at the bottom of the tank. It is possible, where facilities are available, to reactivate return sludge in separate reaeration tanks before addition to the sewage. However, it is much wiser to retain the activity of the sludge by prompt withdrawal from the tank.

Return of the Proper Amount of Activated Sludge for Mixture with the Sewage: The amount of sludge returned to the aeration tank must be sufficient to produce the desired purification in the available aeration time and yet low enough to give economical air utilization. Because of variations in the character and concentration of the sewage and the type of plant, the amount of returned sludge may range from 10 to 15 percent of the volume of sewage being treated. This will be further discussed in connection with the various types of plants. For a conventional plant, the percentage is usually between 20 and 30 percent. This will result in a concentration of solids in the mixed liquor of from 1,000 to 2,500 ppm in diffused air plants, and 500 to 1,500 ppm in mechanical aeration plants. The best concentration must be determined for each plant by trial operator and should be carefully maintained by controlling the proportion of return sludge. The maximum concentration is limited by the air supply and sewage load. If solids are allowed to build up, the air and food requirements will exceed those available and an upset will occur.

Treatment and Disposal of Excess Activated Sludge: Ultimately, excess activated sludge is treated and disposed of with the sludge from primary sedimentation tanks. There are several methods by which excess activated sludge is combined with sludge from primary devices.

Probably the most common practice is to pump excess sludge to the influent end of the primary sedimentation tank where it is settled with the solids in the raw sewage. The activated sludge settles readily and, because of the large flocculent character of the sludge particles, it tends to strain out some of the non-settleable solids in the sewage, thus reducing the organic and solids load on the aeration tank.

Where the above procedure is not followed, the excess activated sludge is transferred to the sludge digestion tanks either directly or through thickeners.

FIGURE 15a
CONVENTIONAL ACTIVATED SLUDGE

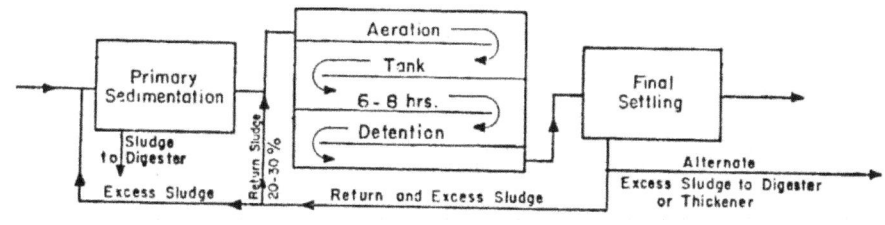

FIGURE 15b
STEP AERATION

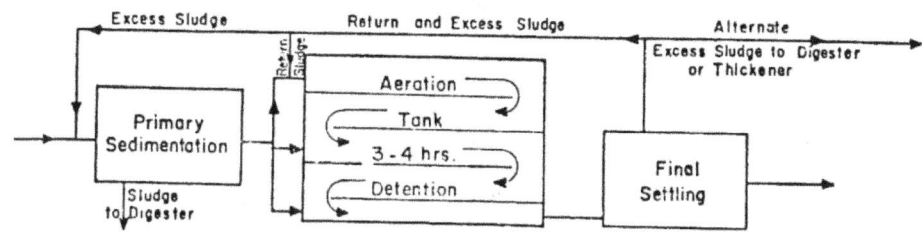

FIGURE 15c
MODIFIED AERATION

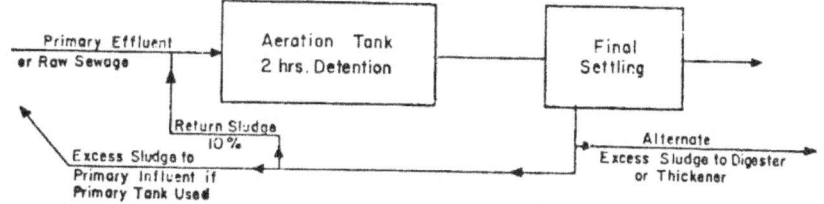

FIGURE 15d
ACTIVATED AERATION

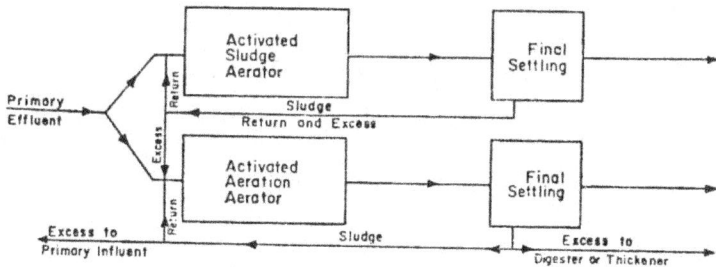

49

Conventional Activated Sludge Process: The flow diagram of a conventional activated sludge plant for domestic sewage using the diffused air system is shown in Figure 15a. All of the settled sewage is mixed with the returned activated sludge at the head of the aeration tank. With average domestic sewage, the volume of returned sludge is 20 to 30 percent of the volume of the sewage to be treated. The aeration tanks are designed to provide an aeration time of six to eight hours with diffused air aeration and nine to twelve hours for mechanical aeration. The longer times are used for the lower sewage flows. Air is applied at the rate of one to one and one-half cubic feet per gallon of sewage or 900 to 1100 cubic feet per pound of BOD to be removed. Activated sludge is returned at a rate to maintain a solids content in the mixed liquor of 1,000 to 2,500 ppm. Sludge index and sludge age, as determined for each plant, will usually fall within the range of 200 to 300 and three to four days, respectively. An overall plant efficiency, as measured by reduction in BOD and suspended solids, of 80 to 90 percent can be expected with efficiencies in the upper part of this range predominating.

The conventional activated sludge process is capable of effecting the highest degree of purification yet attained by sewage treatment methods that are in general use with the exception of that obtained by intermittent sand filtration. Although the activated sludge is similar in composition and biochemical reactions to the slime formed on trickling filter medium, it is somewhat more effective. The activated sludge floc moves through the sewage flow and, in effect, goes searching for food. Consequently, the decomposition of the organic matter in the sewage can be more complete than that which can be attained by trickling filters. Since the biological contact process takes place under water, fly breeding is eliminated and odors can be greatly reduced. The space required for activated sludge units is much less than needed for trickling filters used to treat the same volume of flow.

The activated sludge process is not as rugged, however, as the trickling filter process. It is complex and presents many technical problems requiring more operating skill and time. While the activated sludge process can be adapted to treat sewage and wastes of widely varying strengths and composition, it is sensitive to shock loads and toxic substances which may be discharged into sewers, especially from industrial plants. These industrial wastes may destroy or inhibit the activity of the microorganism essential for the decomposition of organic matter.

MODIFICATIONS OF THE CONVENTIONAL ACTIVATED SLUDGE PROCESS

Mention has already been made of modifications of the conventional activated sludge plant. These have been developed to meet local conditions or to effect economies in construction and operation. Several of these modifications are described below.

Step Aeration: In this process, Figure 15b, sewage enters the aeration tank at a number of different points but all of the return sludge is introduced at the first point of entry with, or without, a portion of the sewage. The sludge solids concentration in the mixed liquor is, therefore, greatest at the first step or point of entry and decreases as more sewage is introduced at subsequent steps. This provides a means of ready regulation of the total amount of solids held under aeration. In this process, treatment practically equivalent to the conventional activates sludge process can be attained in about half the aeration time while maintaining the sludge age within proper limits of three to four days.

By using an aeration tank of only half the capacity needed in the conventional process, construction costs and the area required for step aeration are less. Operation costs are about the same for the conventional and step processes.

Tapered Aeration: This process was developed on the theory that the greatest amount of air is needed during the early part of the aeration period. Air is, therefore, introduced into the sewage at a higher rate in the inlet section of the aeration tank than in subsequent sections to roughly approximate the oxygen utilization in the various sections or stages of aeration in the tank.

The advantages claimed for his modification of the conventional activated sludge process are a better control of the process in meeting shock loads and a reduction in the cost of operation.

Modified Aeration: This modification of the conventional activated sludge process, Figure 15c, is also known as high-rate activated sludge treatment. It is applicable where the receiving waters require a degree of treatment greater than that obtained by primary treatment but not the suspended solids and BOD removals that can be obtained by the conventional activated sludge process.

In modified aeration either raw or settled sewage mixed with about 10 percent of return sludge is aerated for a period of only one or two hours. The suspended solids of the mixed liquor are reduced to below 1,000 ppm resulting in a reduction in air requirements. By controlling the air supply, the aeration period, and the percent of return sludge, almost any degree of treatment between primary sedimentation and the conventional activated sludge process can be effected.

This process effects savings in construction and operating costs and takes less area than the conventional plant. The sludge produced is dense, more nearly resembling primary tank sludge than activated sludge, and is not subject to bulking as described later.

Activated Aeration: This process was recently developed in New York City, Figure 15d, and is a conventional or step-activated sludge treatment with a reduced aeration period. The culture which is produced in the activated sludge section and which is ordinarily wasted as excess sludge, is transferred to an activated aeration section which also receives a portion of the settled sewage flow. In the activated aeration section, that portion of settled sewage sent to it is aerated with a low solids concentration of 200 to 400 ppm. Final settling tanks are provided for both sections with effluents to the receiving waters.

By varying the proportion of the total sewage flow between the two sections of the plant and other operating factors, the activated aeration process affords great flexibility and a wide range of treatment efficiency, depending on the requirement of the receiving waters. Reductions in BOD of 80 to 85 percent can be attained along with savings in air costs as compared with the conventional process.

Contact Stabilization is another modification of the conventional activated sludge process. In this method, the biologically active sludge is brought into intimate contact with the sewage for only 15 to 30 minutes, during which time the activated sludge absorbs and adsorbs a high percentage of the suspended, colloidal, and dissolved pollutional matter from the sewage. The mixture then flows to the settling tank from which the sludge is removed to a regenerating tank where it is stabilized and regenerated by aeration. This modification is especially applicable in treating industrial wastes as the entire supply of seed sludge is not vulnerable to shock loads because the majority of the seed is kept under separate aeration. A slug of wastes would only affect that small portion of the sludge being mixed with the sewage.

Aerobic Digestion (Total Oxidation): In this process, a continuous flow of raw sewage or wastes and its macerated solids are aerated vigorously in a tank designed to detain an entire day's flow. The aerated sewage then passes to a conventional settling tank where two functions occur—clarified effluent overflows to the receiving waters and settled sludge is recirculated back to the aeration compartment at a high rate.

This relatively simple process depends upon practically complete stabilization of the putrescible fraction of the sewage by biological oxidation in a single compartment. Experience indicates that this process is sensitive to sudden changes in volume and/or character of the waste. Sludge should be wasted periodically from the system in order to maintain equilibrium and consistently produce a high quality effluent.

This process has been applied at moderately small installations thus far, and experience indicates that the resultant degree of treatment realized compares favorably with other highly efficient secondary processes.

OPERATION OF ACTIVATED SLUDGE PROCESS

Details of operating procedure will vary at different activated sludge plants, depending on a number of factors, such as the type of facilities available, strength and character of the sewage, temperatures, requirements of receiving waters, and others. Best operating procedure for each plant must be determined by experience. With this qualification, the following will generally apply for a conventional type of plant treating an average domestic sewage. For modified type plants, see the sections on these various units.

1. There must be sufficient aeration to maintain a dissolved oxygen content of at least two ppm at all times throughout the aeration tanks, except immediately beyond the inlet. This can be expected when an aeration time of six to eight hours for diffused air and nine to twelve hours with mechanical aeration is provided and when about 1,000 cubic feet of air is supplied for each pound of BOD to be removed.

2. Dissolved oxygen should be present at all times in the treated sewage in the final settling tanks.

3. Activated sludge must be returned continuously from the final settling tanks to the aeration tanks.

4. Optimum rate of returning activated sludge will vary with each installation and with different load factors. In general, it will range from 20 to 30 percent of the sewage flow for diffused air and 10 to 20 percent for mechanical aeration units.

5. The optimum suspended solids content in the aeration tanks may vary considerably but usually in the range of 1,000 to 2,500 ppm with diffused air and 600 to 1,200 ppm with mechanical aeration.

6. A sludge volume index of about 100 and a sludge age of three to four days are normal for most plants. When the optimum sludge volume index is established for a plant, it should be maintained within a reasonably narrow range. A material increase is a warning of trouble ahead as discussed below under sludge bulking.

7. The suspended solids content in the aeration tanks may be controlled by the amount of sludge returned to them. All sludge in excess of that needed in the aeration tanks must be removed from the system. It should be removed in small amounts continuously or at frequent intervals rather than in large amounts at any one time. Sludge held too long in the final settling tank will become septic, lose its activity, and deplete the necessary dissolved oxygen content in the tank. (See 2 above.)

8. Septic conditions in the primary sedimentation tanks will adversely affect the functioning of the activated sludge process. Pre-chlorination or pre-aeration as described under preliminary treatment in Chapter 4 may be used to forestall septic conditions in the sewage

52

entering the aeration tanks.

9. Periodic or sudden organic overloads, such as may result from large amounts of sludge digester overflow to the primary tanks or from doses of industrial wastes having an excessive BOD or containing toxic chemicals, will usually cause operating difficulties. Whenever possible, overloading should be minimized by controlling the discharge or by pretreatment of such deleterious wastes. It may even be preferable to bypass the activated sludge units at the plant than to knock out the whole activated sludge process. This procedure must be used with caution and if it must become a frequent practice or involves large volumes, the plant facilities are probably inadequate and additional units must be installed.

Sludge Bulking: The most common problem encountered in the operation of activated sludge plants is sludge bulking. A desirable activated sludge is one which settles rapidly leaving a clear, odorless, and stable supernatant. The floc is granular in appearance, with sharp defined edges, is golden brown in color, and has a musty odor. When the character of the activated sludge changes so that its settleability decreases, as measured by a significant rise in the sludge volume index, a condition known as sludge bulking develops in the final settling tank. As a portion of the sludge does not settle in the tank, it is carried away in the effluent. This results in a serious impairment in the quality of the plant effluent and places an added organic load on the receiving waters.

As always, it is better, where possible, to prevent trouble than to correct it, and knowledge of its possible source is the first step in prevention. There are a number of causes for sludge bulking, some of which are given below.

1. Excessive or storm flow resulting in shortened aeration periods

2. Short circuiting of aeration tanks

3. Industrial wastes with high organic content or containing chemicals having toxic effects on bacteria development.

4. Solids content in aeration tanks either too high or too low.

5. Insufficient aeration with failure to maintain dissolved oxygen throughout the system or possibly the use of too much air tending to break up the floc

6. Septic sewage in the primary sedimentation

7. Interruption in the continuity of returning of sludge to the aeration tank or too long intervals in removing excess sludge from the process units.

8. A preponderance of fungi forming thread-like filaments in the sludge.

All of these can be pretty well summed up by saying that sludge bulking results from overloading or the improper balance between the three variable—BOD loading, suspended solids concentration of the mixed liquor, and the amount of air used in aeration.

There are no infallible rules for either the prevention or control of sludge bulking. If the condition does develop, the ultimate solution is to determine the cause and then either correct or eliminate it or take compensatory steps in operation control. There are some remedial steps which can be taken where facilities are available, and which may help to bring the process back to normal operation. Among these are:

1. Addition of hydrated lime to the aeration tanks to raise the pH value to not exceeding 7.1. This was formerly used more than at present. It has been largely replaced by the use of chlorine as noted under 4 below.

2. Reduction of the solids content carried in aeration tanks by removal of some of the activated sludge as excess.

3. Re-aeration of returned activated sludge before entering aeration tanks.

4. Chlorination of returned activated sludge. This must be carefully controlled to avoid killing the organisms in the sludge.

5. Increase aeration in time and rate.

It is sometimes desirable or necessary to remove as much of the sludge as possible from the system and then develop fresh and properly activated sludge.

Frothing: The formation of a thick layer of froth over the surface of aeration tanks is becoming a more common and more serious problem for the operators of activates sludge plants. The cause (or causes) are not definitely known, though it is frequently attributed to the increasing use in industry and homes of synthetic detergent compounds. Whatever the cause, there are several methods of control available. One method is the use of defoamants which tend to reduce surface tension and are quite effective. These materials are expensive and cost may prevent their use when large quantities are required. Another method is the application to the foam of fine sprays of water or plant effluent. The installation and operation of a satisfactory spray system may also involve considerable expenditures. At some plants a combination of these two methods has been used by adding a defoamant to the spray. The necessity for foam control and the control method used depend on the seriousness of the problem and the relative costs of the various control methods at any specific plant.

CONTACT AERATION

The contact aeration process is covered by several patents. Like all secondary treatment processes, it depends on aerobic biological organisms to break down the complex putrescible organic material in sewage into simpler, more stable forms. The organisms are, like those in a trickling filter, stationary and attached to a fixed medium. They are, however, continually submerged and supplied with air by means similar to the diffused air system in the activated sludge process.

A typical contact aeration plant consists of five tanks in series to provide for primary settling, first stage aeration, intermediate settling, second stage aeration, and final settling. In addition, facilities for sludge treatment and disposal must be provided.

The aeration units consist of tanks which contain a number of thin plates made of a variety of materials such as corrugated aluminum sheets or corrugated asbestos sheets. These are suspended vertically and spaced about one and one-half inch center to center. The necessary biological life develops on these sheets. Sewage is carried to the bottom of the tank and passes upward between the plates mixed with air from a diffuser system at the bottom. Aerobic conditions are thus maintained for the biological life on the submerged plates. Growths with organic solids are continually breaking away from the plates. Those from first stage aeration are removed in the intermediate settling tanks and those from second stage aeration in the final settling tank.

The process is quite rugged and can, like the trickling filter, withstand shock loads. The units are adaptable to manufacture and installation as "package" units with automatic controls to reduce, but not eliminate, the time and attention given to operation. A removal of BOD and suspended solids of 90 percent or more can be attained with plants correctly designed and operated. To date, the use of this process has been restricted to plants serving small villages, realty developments or similar small groups. However, with multiple units, larger installations would appear to be practical.

INTERMITTENT SAND FILTERS

The intermittent sand filter is a specially prepared bed of sand on which effluents from primary treatment or from trickling filters or secondary settling tanks may be applied intermittently by using troughs or perforated pipe distributors. The effluent from the filter is removed by an underdrainage system.

Bed Construction: The filter bed should have a depth of clean sand of at least 24 inches overlying clean, graded gravel. The gravel should be placed in at least three layers around the underdrains and to a depth of at least six inches over the top of the underdrains. The sand itself should have an effective size of 0.3 to 0.6 millimeters and have a uniformity coefficient of not more than 3.5. The center to center spacing of underdrains should not be more than 10 feet.

Capacity: When treating a primary effluent from normal sewage, the rate of application on the filter should not exceed 125,000 gallons per acre per day, which should be reduced if the sewage is strong. With trickling filter and secondary settling tank effluent, the loading should not exceed 500,000 gallons per acre per day.

The intermittent sand filter is a true filter which strains out and retains fine suspended solids and also acts as an oxidizing unit. The major portion of the straining and oxidation is effected at or near the surface of the sand. Straining results from the fine nature of the sand medium with small voids and from a biological slime growth of organisms which develops on the surface of the sand. Oxidation is effected, as in all secondary treatment devices, by the living aerobic microorganisms which develop primarily at the surface, forming a slime layer, but also extending into the sane medium.

Operation: It is important that the filter be allowed to empty itself and obtain a fresh air supply at intervals. This is accomplished by intermittent dosing of the sewage onto the filter. Sewage is applied from two to six times a day in quantities sufficient to cover the surface of the filter to a depth of two to three inches; and as the sewage passes down through the sand, air is drawn in from the surface. Sand filters are constructed in two or more units which are used in rotation. Eventually, the slime layer on the surface causes the top layer of sand to become clogged and necessitates the removal of the top layer of sand in order to put the unit back into efficient operation.

Pooling should not be allowed to develop on the beds as this tends to produce septic action, obnoxious odors, and an effluent of poor quality. Pooling indicates that cleaning is necessary. The surface of the beds should be kept level to afford uniform distribution of the sewage and weeds, grass, etc. and should not be allowed to grow on the beds.

For winter use, the open air beds in the northern part of the state should be ridged every two feet in order to hold the ice off the main body of sand. An alternate method is that of raking up small four to six inch piles of the top surface every three feet over the surface of the bed. The bed should be cleaned and leveled as early as possible in the spring. Where natural sand percolation beds are used, it is sometimes advisable to shallow harrow the beds after careful removal of all organic deposits. Such harrowing is not advisable with underdrained beds because of possible damage to the underdraining system.

Efficiency and Use: A well operated intermittent sand filter plant will give a clear, sparkling stable effluent almost completely oxidized and nitrified. Overall plant removals of 95 percent or more of the BOD and suspended solids in the raw sewage can be expected. This exceeds other accepted secondary treatment processes.

When compared with other sewage treatment processes, large areas of land are needed, construction costs per unit of sewage treated are high, and maintenance in keeping filters clean is considerable. The use of filters of this type is restricted to situations where the volume of sewage to be treated is small, or where an exceptionally high grade of plant effluent is necessary. They have been used effectively for the additional treatment of secondary treatment effluents. Modification of the sand filters have been proposed in the past but, in general, have not proven practical for treatment of large volumes of sewage.

STABILIZATION PONDS

In recent years there has developed a system of sewage treatment which depends on the use of specially prepared ponds which are termed *stabilization ponds*. These ponds were first used in areas where warm climates and sunny days are prevalent, but have been found to operate with satisfactory results in colder climates and where there is considerable cloudiness. Stabilization ponds might be used most anywhere. The rate at which they could be operated would vary with temperature, light energy, and other local conditions.

The process involves two steps in the decomposition of organic matter in sewage. The carbonaceous matter in sewage is first broken down by the aerobic organisms with the formation of carbon dioxide. The carbon dioxide so formed is used by algae in their photosynthesis. *Photosynthesis* is a natural process carried on in green plant tissue under the influence of light and in the presence of chlorophyll which is the green coloring substance of plant life. In this process, the oxygen in the carbon dioxide is liberated and dissolved by the liquid in which the algae grow. As a result, the organic matter in sewage is converted into algae and the sewage is supplied with oxygen to support further aerobic decomposition. The sewage solids enter the pond in a highly putrescible state and leave in the form of highly stable algae cells which, within certain limitations, can be discharged to receiving waters without deleterious effect.

Oxidation ponds can be used as a complete treatment receiving raw sewage, or as a secondary treatment for settled sewage, or as a further treatment for effluents from secondary processes. They have been used most commonly as a secondary treatment for primary effluents.

Most stabilization ponds are two to four feet in depth with continuous flow through the pond. They have been designed for loadings of one acre per 400 persons, 50 pounds of BOD per acre per day or 15 pounds of BOD per acre foot per day with detention periods generally greater than 30 days. The natural soil in which they are located should be fairly impervious, so that seepage will not materially affect the surface level of the sewage in the pond.

These ponds are low cost in construction, and require a minimum of operation. The requirement that large, fairly isolated areas be provided limits their use to relatively small populations in areas where land is available.

GLOSSARY OF SEWAGE TREATMENT TERMS

CONTENTS

	Page
Activated Sludge Process……………………Arrester, Flame	1
Bacteria……………………………………Burner, Waste Gas	2
Centrifuge…………………………………………..Chlorine	3
Clarifier……………………………………………Digestion	4
Dilution……………………………………………..Effluent	5
Ejector, Pneumatic…………………………………... Floc	6
Flocculator………………………………………….. Grease	7
Grinder, Screenings………………………………..Impeller	8
Index, Sludge Volume………………………..…….Mold	9
Most Probable Number, (MPN)……………….…... Period	10
pH……………………………………………………..Pump	11
Purification…………………………………………….Rate	12
Reaeration………………………………….Sedimentation	13
Seeding, Sludge……………………………………..Sewer	14
Sewerage……………………………………………Solids	15
Squeegee………………………………………...Treatment	16
Trap, Flame……………………………………….Zooglea	17

GLOSSARY OF SEWAGE TREATMENT TERMS

A

Activated Sludge Process.—See **Process, Activated Sludge.**

Acre-Foot.—A unit of volume used to express the amount of material in a trickling filter. A depth of one foot on an area of one acre is an acre-foot. Regardless of shape, 43,560 cubic feet is equivalent to one acre foot.

Adsorption.—The adherence of dissolved, colloidal, or finely divided solids on the surfaces of solid bodies with which they are brought into contact.

Aeration.—The bringing about of intimate contact between air and a liquid by one of the following methods: Spraying the liquid in the air; or by agitation of the liquid to promote surface absorption of air.

    Diffused Air.—Aeration produced in a liquid by air passed through a diffuser.

    Mechanical.— (1) The mixing, by mechanical means, of sewage and activated sludge, in the aeration tank of the activated sludge process, to bring fresh surfaces of liquid into contact with the atmosphere. (2) The introduction of atmospheric oxygen into a liquid by the mechanical action of paddle or spray mechanisms.

    Modified.—A modification of the activated sludge process in which a shortened period of aeration is employed with a reduced quantity of suspended solids in the mixed liquor.

    Paddle-Wheel.—The mechanical agitation of sewage in the aeration tanks of the activated sludge process by means of paddle wheels.

    Spiral Flow.—A method of diffusing air in an aeration tank of the activated sludge process, where, by means of properly designed baffles, and the proper location of diffusers, a spiral or helical movement is given to the air and the tank liquor.

    Stage.—Division of activated sludge treatment into stages with intermediate settling tanks and return of sludge in each stage.

    Step.—A procedure for adding increments of sewage along the line of flow in the aeration tanks of an activated sludge plant.

    Tapered.—The method of supplying varying amounts of air into the different parts of an aeration tank in the activated sludge process, more at the inlet, less near the outlet, and approximately proportional to the oxygen demand of the mixed liquor under aeration.

Algae.—Primitive plants, one or many-celled, usually aquatic and capable of elaborating their foodstuffs by photosynthesis.

Algicide.—Any substance which kills algae.

Alkaline.—Water or soils containing sufficient amounts of alkaline substances to raise the pH above 7.0, or to harm the growth of crops.

Alkalinity.—A term used to represent the content of carbonates, bicarbonates, hydroxides, and occasionally borates, silicates, and phosphates in water. It is expressed in parts per million of calcium carbonate.

Alum.—A common name for aluminum sulfate.

Arrester, Flame.—A safety device on a gas line which allows gas, but not a flame, to pass through.

B

Bacteria.—Primitive plants, generally free of pigment, which reproduce by dividing in one, two, or three planes. They occur as single cells, groups, chains, or filaments, and do not require light for their life processes. They may be grown by special culturing out of their native habitat.

    Aerobic.—Bacteria which require free (elementary) oxygen for their growth.

    Anaerobic.—Bacteria which grow in the absence of free oxygen and derive oxygen from breaking down complex substances.

    Coli-Aerogenes.—See Bacteria, Coliform Group.

    Coliform Group.—A group of bacteria, predominantly inhabitants of the intestine of man but also found on vegetation, including all aerobic and facultative anaerobic grain-negative, non-spore-forming bacilli that ferment lactose with gas formation. This group includes five tribes of which the very great majority are Eschericheae. The Eschericheae tribe comprises three genera and ten species, of which *Escherichia Coli* and *Aerobacter Aerogenes* are dominant. *The Escherichia Coli* are normal inhabitants of the intestine of man and all vertebrates whereas Aerobacter Aerogenes normally are found on grain and plants, and only to a varying degree in the intestine of man and animals. Formerly referred to as *B.Coli*, B.Coli group, *ColiAerogenes Group*.

    Facultative Anaerobic.—Bacteria which can adapt themselves to growth in the presence, as well as in the absence, of uncombined oxygen.

    Parasitic.—Bacteria which thrive on other living organisms.

    Pathogenic.—Bacteria which can cause disease.

    Saprophytic.—Bacteria which thrive upon dead organic matter.

Bacterial Count.—A measure of the concentration of bacteria.

    Most Probable Number.—See Page 10.

    Plate.—Number of colonies of bacteria grown on selected solid media at a given temperature and incubation period, usually expressed as the number of bacteria per milliliter of sample.

Bed, Sludge.—An area comprising natural or artificial layers of porous material upon which digested sewage sludge is dried by drainage and evaporation. A sludge bed may be opened to the atmosphere or covered usually with a greenhouse-type superstructure. Also called Sludge Drying Bed.

Biochemical.—Resulting from biologic growth or activity, and measured by or expressed in terms of the ensuing chemical change.

Biochemical Action.—Chemical changes resulting from the metabolism of living organisms.

Biochemical Oxygen Demand (BOD).—The quantity of oxygen utilized in the biochemical oxidation of organic matter in a specified time and at a specified temperature. It is not related to the oxygen requirements in chemical combustion, being determined entirely by the availability of the material as a biological food and by the amount of oxygen utilized by the microorganisms during oxidation.

Biochemical Oxygen Demand, Standard.—Biochemical oxygen demand as determined under standard laboratory procedure for five days at 20°C, usually expressed in parts per million.

Buffer.—The action of certain solutions in opposing a change of composition, especially of hydrogen-ion concentration.

Burner, Waste Gas.—A device in a sewage treatment plant for burning the waste gas from a sludge-digestion tank.

C

Centrifuge.—A mechanical device utilizing centrifugal force to separate solids from liquids or for separating liquid emulsions.

Chamber.—A general term applied to a space enclosed by walls or to a compartment, often prefixed by a descriptive word, such as "grit chamber," "screen chamber," "discharge chamber," or "flushing chamber," indicating its function.

Chloramines.—Compounds of organic amines or inorganic ammonia with chlorine.

Chloride of Lime.—Obsolete term; see Chlorinated Lime.

Chlorinated Lime.—A combination of slaked lime and chlorine gas (also termed Bleaching Powder, Chloride of Lime, Hypochlorite of Lime, etc.). When dissolved in water, it serves as a source of chlorine.

Chlorination.—The application of chlorine.

  Break-Point.—The application of chlorine to water, sewage or industrial wastes containing free ammonia to provide free residual chlorination.

  Post.—The application of chlorine to water, sewage, or industrial wastes subsequent to any treatment. The term refers only to a point of application.

  Pre.—The application of chlorine to water, sewage, or industrial wastes prior to any treatment. This term refers only to a point of application.

Chlorine.—An element, when uncombined, exists as a greenish yellow gas about 2.5 times as heavy as air. Under atmospheric pressure and at a temperature of —30.1°F the gas becomes an amber liquid about 1.5 times as heavy as water. The chemical symbol of chlorine is Cl, UP atomic weight is 35.457, and its molecular weight is 70.914.

  Available.—A term used in rating chlorinated lime and hypochlorites as to their total oxidizing power.

  Combined Available Residual.—That portion of the total residual chlorine remaining in water, sewage, or industrial wastes at the end of a specified contact period, which will react chemically and biologically as chloramines, or organic chloramines.

  Demand.—The difference between the amount of chlorine added to water, sewage, or industrial wastes and the amount of residual chlorine remaining at the end of a specified contact period. The demand for any given water varies with the amount of chlorine applied, time of contact, and temperas pure.

  Dose.—The amount of chlorine applied to a liquid, usually expressed in parts per million, or pounds per million gallons.

  Free Available Residual.—That portion of the total residual chlorine remaining in water. sewage, or industrial wastes at the end of a specified contact period. which will react chemically and biologically as hypochlorous acid, hypochlorite ion, or molecular chlorine.

  Liquid.—An article of commerce. Chlorine gas is generally manufactured by the electrolysis of a solution of common salt. The gas is dried and purified and is then liquefied by a combination of compression and refrigeration. Liquid chlorine is shipped under pressure in steel containers.

  Residual.--The total amount of chlorine (combined and free available chlorine) remaining in water, sewage, or industrial wastes at the end of a specified contact period following chlorination.

  Test, Iodometric.—The determination of residual chlorine in water, sewage, or industrial wastes by adding potassium iodide and titrating the liberated iodine with a standard solution of sodium thiosulfate, using starch solution as a colorimetric indicator.

Test, Ortho-Tolidine.—The determination of residual chlorine in water, sewage, or industrial wastes, using ortho-tolidine reagent and colorimetric standards.

Clarifier.—See Tank, Sedimentation.

Coagulation.—(1) The agglomeration of colloidal or finely divided suspended matter by the addition to the liquid of an appropriate chemical coagulant, by biological processes, or by other means. (2) The process of adding a coagulant and the necessary reacting chemicals.

Coils, Digester.—A system of pipes for hot water or steam installed in a sludge-digestion tank for the purpose of heating the sludge.

Coli-Aerogenes, or Coliform Group.—See Bacteria, Coliform Group.

Collector, Grit.—A device placed in a grit chamber to convey deposited grit to one end of the chamber for removal.

    Scum.—A mechanical device for skimming and removing scum from the surface of settling tanks.

    Sludge.—A mechanical device for scraping the sludge on the bottom of a settling tank to a sump, from which it can be drawn by hydrostatic or mechanical action.

Colloids.—Finely divided solids which will not settle but may be removed by coagulation or biochemical action.

Comminution.—The process of screening sewage and cutting the screenings into particles sufficiently fine to pass through the screen openings.

Concentration, Hydrogen-Ion.—See pH.

Copperas.—A common name for ferrous sulfate.

Copperas, Chlorinated.—A solution of ferrous sulfate and ferric chloride produced by chlorinating a solution of ferrous sulfate.

Cross Connection.—In plumbing, a physical connection through which a supply of potable water could be contaminated, polluted, or infected. A physical connection between water supplies from different systems.

Cubic Foot per Second.—A unit of discharge for measurement of flowing liquid, equal to a flow of one cubic foot per second past a given section. Also called Second-Foot.

D

Decomposition of Sewage.—The breakdown of the organic matter in sewage through aerobic and anaerobic processes.

Denitrification.—The reduction of nitrates in solution by biochemical action.

Deoxygenation.—The depletion of the dissolved oxygen in a liquid. Under natural conditions associated with the biochemical oxidation of organic matter present.

Detritus.—The sand, grit, and other coarse material removed by differential sedimentation in a relatively short period of detention.

Diffuser.—A porous plate or tube through which air is forced and divided into minute bubbles for diffusion in liquids. Commonly made of carborundum, alundum, or silica sand.

Digester.—A tank in which the solids resulting from the sedimentation of sewage are stored for the purpose of permitting anaerobic decomposition to the point of rendering the product nonputrescible and inoffensive. Erroneously termed digestor.

Digestion.—The processes occurring in a digester.

    Mesophilic.—Digestion by biological action at or below 113°F.

    Separate Sludge.—The digestion of sludge in separate tanks in which it is placed after it has been allowed to settle in other tanks.

Single-Stage Sludge.—Sludge digestion limited to a single tank for the entire digestion period.

Stage.—The digestion of sludge progressively in several tanks arranged in series.

Thermophilic.—Digestion carried on at a temperature generally between 113°F and 145°F.

Dilution. — (1) A method of disposing of sewage, industrial waste, or sewage treatment plant effluent by discharging it into a stream or body of water. (2) The ratio of volume of flow of a stream to the total volume of sewage or sewage treatment, ant effluent discharged into it.

Disinfection.—The killing of the larger portion (but not necessarily all) of the harmful and objectional microorganisms in, or on, a medium by means of chemicals, heat, ultraviolet light, etc.

Distributor.—A device used to apply liquid to the surface of a filter or contact bed, of two general types, fixed o movable. The fixed type may consist of perforated pipes or notched troughs, sloping boards, or sprinkler nozzles. The movable type may consist of rotating disks or rotating, reciprocating, or traveling perforated pipes or troughs applying a spray, or a thin sheet of liquid.

Dosing Tank.—A tank into which raw or partly treated sewage is introduced and held until the desired quantity has been accumulated, after which it is discharged at such a rate as may be necessary for the subsequent treatment.

Dryer.—A device utilizing heat to remove water.

Flash.—A device for vaporizing water from partly dewatered and finely divided sludge through contact with a current of hot gas or superheated vapor. Included is a squirrel cage mill for separating the sludge cake into fine particles.

Rotary.—A long steel cylinder, slowly revolving, with its long axis slightly inclined, through which passes the material to be dried in hot air. The material passes through from inlet to outlet, tumbling about.

E

E. Coli.—(Escherichia Coli).—A species of genus Escherichia bacteria, normal inhabitant of the intestine of man and all vertebrates. This species is classified among the Coliform Group. See Bacteria, Coliform Group.

Efficiency.—The ratio of the actual performance of a device to the theoretically perfect performance usually expressed as a percentage.

Average.—The efficiency of a machine or mechanical device over the range of load through which the machine operates.

Filter.—The operating results from a filter as measured by various criteria such as percentage reduction in suspended matter, total solids, biochemical oxygen demand, bacteria, color, etc.

Pump.—The ratio of energy converted into useful work to the energy applied to the pump shaft, or the energy difference in the water at the discharge and suction nozzles divided by the energy input at the pump shaft.

Wire-to-Water.—The ratio of the mechanical output of a pump, to the electrical input at the meter.

Effluent.—(1) A liquid which flows out of a containing space. (2) Sewage, water, or other liquid, partially or completely treated, or in its natural state, as the case may be, flowing out of a reservoir, basin, or treatment plant, or part thereof.

Final.—The effluent from the final unit of a sewage treatment plant.

Stable.—A treated sewage which contains enough oxygen to satisfy its oxygen demand.

Ejector, Pneumatic.—A device for raising sewage, sludge, or other liquid by alternately admitting such through an inward swinging check valve into the bottom of an airtight pot and then discharging it through an outward swinging check valve by admitting compressed air to the pot above the liquid.

Elutriation.—A process of sludge conditioning in which certain constituents are removed by successive decantations with fresh water or plant effluent, thereby reducing the demand for conditioning chemicals.

F

Factor.—Frequently a ratio used to express operating conditions.
  Load.—The ratio of the average load carried by any operation to the maximum load carried, during a given period of time, expressed as a percentage. The load may consist of almost anything, such as electrical power, number of persons served, amount of water carried by a conduit, etc.
  Power.—An electrical term describing the ratio of the true power passing through an electric circuit to the product of the volts times the amperes in the circuit. It is a measure of the lag or lead of the current in respect to the voltage. While the power of a current is the product of the voltage times the amperes in the circuit, in alternating current the voltage and amperes are not always in phase, hence the true power may be less than that determined by the product of volts times amperes.

Filter.—A term meaning (1) an oxidizing bed (2) a device for removing solids from a liquid by some type of strainer.
  Biological.—A bed of sand, gravel, broken stone, or other media through which sewage flows or trickles, which depends on biological action for its effectiveness.
  High-Rate.—A trickling filter operated at a high average daily dosing rate usually between 10-30 mgd per acre, sometimes including recirculation of effluent.
  Low-Rate.—A trickling filter designed to receive a small load of BOD per unit volume of filtering material and to have a low dosage rate per unit of surface area (usually 1 to 4 mgd per acre). Also called Standard Rate Filter.
  Roughing.—A sewage filter of relatively coarse material operated at a high rate as a preliminary treatment.
  Sand.—A filter in which sand is used as a filtering medium.
  Sand Sludge.—A bed of sand used to dewater sludge by drainage and evaporation.
  Sludge.—The solid matter in sewage that is removed by settling in primary and secondary settling tanks.
  Trickling.—A treatment unit consisting of a material such as broken stone, clinkers, slate, slats, or brush, over which sewage is distributed and applied in drops, films, or spray, from troughs, drippers, moving distributors, or fixed nozzles, and through which it trickles to the underdrains, giving opportunity for the formation of zoological slimes which clarify and oxidize the sewage.
  Vacuum.—A filter consisting of a cylindrical drum mounted on a horizontal axis, covered with filtering material made of wool, felt, cotton, saran, nylon, dacron, polyethylene or similar substance, by stainless steel coil springs or metal screen, revolving with a partial submergence in the liquid. A vacuum is maintained under the cloth for the larger part of a revolution to extract moisture. The cake is scraped off continuously.

Filtrate.—The effluent of a Filter.

Floc.—Small gelatinous masses, formed in a liquid by the addition of coagulants thereto or through biochemical processes or by agglomeration.

Flocculator.—An apparatus for the formation of floc in water or sewage.
Flotation.—A method of raising suspended matter to the surface of the liquid in a tank as scum—by aeration, by the evolution of gas, chemicals, electrolysis, heat, or bacterial decomposition—and the subsequent removal of the scum by skimming.
Freeboard.—The vertical distance between the normal maximum level of the surface of the liquid in a conduit, reservoir, tank, canal, etc., and the top of the sides of an open conduit, the top of a dam or levee, etc., which is provided so that waves and other movements of the liquid will not overtop the confining structure.
Fungi.—Small nonchlorophyll-bearing plants which lack roots, stems, or leaves and which occur (among other places) in water, sewage, or sewage effluents, growing best in the absence of light. Their decomposition after death may cause disagreeable tastes and odors in water; in some sewage treatment processes they are helpful and in others they are detrimental.

G

Gage.—A device for measuring any physical magnitude.
    Float.—A device for measuring the elevation of the surface of a liquid, the actuation element being a buoyant float which rests upon the surface of the liquid.
    Indicator.—A gage that shows by means of an index, pointer, dial, etc., the instantaneous value of such characteristics as depth, pressure, velocity, stage, discharge, or the movements or positions of water-controlling devices.
    Mercury.—A gage wherein pressure of a fluid is measured by the height of a column of mercury which the fluid pressure will sustain. The mercury is usually contained in a tube, attached to the vessel or pipe containing the fluid.
    Pressure.—A device for registering the pressure of solids, liquids, or gases. It may be graduated to the register pressure in any units desired.
Garbage, Ground.—Garbage shredded or ground by apparatus installed in sinks and discharged to the sewerage system; or garbage collected and hauled to a central grinding station, shredded preliminary to disposal, usually, by digestion with sewage sludge.
Gas.—One of the three states of matter.
    Sewage.—(1) The gas produced by the septicization of sewage. (2) The gas produced during the digestion of sewage sludge, usually collected and utilized.
    Sewer.—Gas evolved in sewers from the decomposition of the organic matter in the sewage. Also any gas present in the sewerage system, even though it is from gas mains, gasoline, cleaning fluid, etc.
Gasification.—The transformation of sewage solids into gas in the decomposition of sewage.
Go Devil.—A scraper with self-adjusting spring blades, inserted in a pipe line, and carried forward by the fluid pressure for clearing away accumulations, tuberculations, etc.
Grade.—(1) The inclination or slope of a stream channel, conduit, or natural ground surface, usually expressed in terms of the ratio or percentage of number of units of vertical rise or fall per unit of horizontal distance. (2) The elevation of the invert of the bottom of a pipe line, canal, culvert, sewer, etc. (3) The finished surface of a canal bed, road bed, top of an embankment. or bottom of an excavation. (4) In plumbing, the fall in inches per foot of length of pipe.
Grease.—In sewage, grease including fats, waxes, free fatty acids, calcium and magnesium soaps, mineral oils, and other non-fatty materials. The type of solvent used for its extraction should be stated.

Grinder, Screenings.—A device for grinding, shredding, or comminuting material removed from sewage by screens.

Grit.—The heavy mineral matter in water or sewage, such as gravel, cinders, etc.

H

Head.—Energy per unit weight of liquid at a specified point. It is expressed in feet.

Dynamic.—The head against which a pump works.

Friction.—The head lost by water flowing in a stream or conduit as the result of the disturbances set up by the contact between the moving water and its containing conduit, and by intermolecular friction. In laminar flow the head lost is approximately proportional to the first power of the velocity; in turbulent flow to a higher power, approximately the square of the velocity. While strictly speaking, head losses due to bends, expansions, obstructions, impact, etc., are not included in this term, the usual practice is to include all such head losses under this term.

Loss of.—The decrease in head between two points.

Static.—The vertical distance between the free level of the source of supply, and the point of free discharge, or the level of the free surface.

Total Dynamic.—The difference between the elevation corresponding to the pressure at the discharge flange of a pump and the elevation corresponding to the vacuum or pressure at the suction flange of the pump, corrected to the same datum plane, plus the velocity head at the discharge flange of the pump, minus the velocity head at the suction flange of the pump. It includes the friction head.

Velocity.—The theoretical vertical height through which a liquid body may be raised due to its kinetic energy. It is equal to the square of the velocity divided by twice the acceleration due to gravity.

Humus.—The dark or black carboniferous residue in the soil resulting from the decomposition of vegetable tissues of plants originally growing therein. Residues similar in appearance and behavior are found in well-digested sludges and in activated sludge.

Hypochlorite.—Compounds of chlorine in which the radical (OC1) is present. They are usually inorganic.

High Test.—A solid triple salt containing Ca (OC1) 2 to the extent that the fresh solid has approximately 70 percent available chlorine. It is not the same as chlorinated lime.

Sodium.—A solution containing NaOC1, prepared by passing chlorine into solutions of soda ash, or reacting soda ash solutions with high-test hypochlorites and decanting from the precipitated sludge.

I

Imhoff Cone.—A conically shaped graduated glass vessel used to measure approximately the volume of settleable solids in various liquids of sewage origin.

Imhoff Tank.—See Tank, Imhoff

Impeller.—The rotating part of a centrifugal pump, containing the curved vanes.

Closed.—An impeller having the side walls extended from the outer circumference of the suction opening to the vane tips.

Nonclogging.—An impeller of the open, closed, or semi-closed type designed with large passages for passing large solids.

Open.—An impeller without attached side walls.
Screw.—The helical impeller of a screw pump.

Index, Sludge Volume.—The volume is milliliters occupied by one gram of dry solids after the aerated mixed liquor settles 30 minutes, commonly referred to as the Mohlman index.

Influent.—Sewage, water, or other liquid, raw or partly treated, flowing into a reservoir, basin, or treatment plant, or part thereof.

L

Lagoon, Sludge.—A relatively shallow basin, or natural depression, used for the storage or digestion of sludge, and sometimes for its ultimate detention or dewatering.

Lift, Air.—A device for raising liquid by injecting air in and near the bottom of a riser pipe submerged in the liquid to be raised.

Liquefaction.—The changing of the organic matter in sewage from an insoluble to a soluble state, and effecting a reduction in its solid contents.

Liquor.—Any liquid.

Mixed.—A mixture of activated sludge and sewage in the aeration tank undergoing activated sludge treatment.

Supernatant. — (1) The liquor overlying deposited solids. (2) The liquid in a sludge-digestion tank which lies between the sludge at the bottom and the floating scum at the top.

Loading.—The time rate at which material is applied to a treatment device involving length, area, or volume or other design factor.

BOD, Filter.—The pounds of oxygen demand in the applied liquid per unit of filter bed area, or volume of stone per day.

Weir.—Gallons overflow per day per foot of weir length.

M

Main, Force.—A pipe line on the discharge side of a water or sewage pumping station, usually under pressure.

Manometer.—An instrument for measuring pressure; usually it consists of a U-shaped tube containing a liquid, the surface of which in one end of the tube moves proportionally with changes in pressure upon the liquid in the other end. The term is also applied to a tube type of differential pressure gage.

Matter.—Solids, liquids, and gases.

Inorganic.—Chemical substances of mineral origin. They are not usually volatile with heat.

Organic.—Chemical substances of animal, vegetable and industrial origin. They include most carbon compounds, combustible and volatile with heat.

Suspended.—(1) Solids in suspension in sewage or effluent. (2) Commonly used for solids in suspension in sewage or effluent which can readily be removed by filtering in a laboratory.

Microorganism.—Minute organisms either plant or animal, invisible or barely visible to the naked eye.

Moisture, Percentage.—The water content of sludge expressed as the ratio of the loss in weight after drying at 103°C, to the original weight of the sample, multiplied by one hundred.

Mold.—See Fungi.

Most Probable Number, (MPN).—In the testing of bacterial density by the dilution method, that number of organisms per unit volume which, in accordance with statistical theory, would be more likely than any other possible number to yield the observed test result or which would yield the observed test result with the greatest frequency. Expressed as density of organisms per 100 ml.

N

Nitrification.—The oxidation of ammonia nitrogen into nitrates through biochemical action.

O

Overflow Rate.—One of the criteria for the design of settling tanks in treatment plants; expressed in gallons per day per square foot of surface area in the settling tank. See Surface Settling Rate.

Oxidation.—The addition of oxygen, removal of hydrogen, or the increase in the valence of an element.

    Biochemical.—See Oxidation, Sewage.

    Biological.—See Oxidation, Sewage.

    Direct.—Oxidation of substances in sewage without the benefit of living organisms, by the direct application of air or oxidizing agents such as chlorine.

    Sewage.—The process whereby, through the agency of living organisms in the presence of oxygen, the organic matter contained in sewage is converted into a more stable form.

Oxygen.—A chemical element.

    Available.—The quantity of uncombined or free oxygen dissolved in the water of a stream.

    Balance.—The relation between the biochemical oxygen demand of a sewage or treatment plant effluent and the oxygen available in the diluting water.

    Consumed.—The quantity of oxygen taken from potassium permanganate in solution by a liquid containing organic matter. Commonly regarded as an index of the carbonaceous matter present. Time and temperature must be specified. The chemical oxygen demand (COD) uses potassium dichromate.

    Deficiency.—The additional quantity of oxygen required to satisfy the biochemical oxygen demand in a given liquid. Usually expressed in parts per million.

    Dissolved.—Usually designated as DO. The oxygen dissolved in sewage, water or other liquid usually expressed in parts per million or percent of saturation.

    Residual.—The dissolved oxygen content of a stream after deoxygenation has begun.

    Sag.—A curve that represents the profile of dissolved oxygen content along the course of a stream, resulting from deoxygenation associated with biochemical oxidation of organic matter, and reoxygenation through the absorption of atmospheric oxygen and through biological photosynthesis.

P

Parts Per Million.—Milligrams per liter expressing the concentration of a specified component in a dilute sewage. A ratio of pounds per million pounds, grams per million grams, etc.

Percolation.—The flow or trickling of a liquid downward through a contact or filtering medium. The liquid may or may not fill the pores of the medium.

Period.—A time interval.

Aeration.—(1) The theoretical time, usually expressed in hours that the mixed liquor is subjected to aeration in an aeration tank undergoing activated sludge treatment; is equal to (a) the volume of the tank divided by (b) the volumetric rate of flow of the sewage and return sludge. (2) The theoretical time that water is subjected to aeration.

Detention.—The theoretical time required to displace the contents of a tank or unit at a given rate of discharge (volume divided by rate of discharge).

Flowing-Through.—The average time required for a small unit volume of liquid to pass through a basin from inlet to outlet. In a tank where there is no short-circuiting, and no spaces, the detention period and the flowing-through period are the same.

pH.—The logarithm of the reciprocal of the hydrogen-ion concentration. It is not the same as the alkalinity and cannot be calculated therefrom.

Plankton.—Drifting organisms, usually microscopic.

Pollution.—The addition of sewage, industrial wastes, or other harmful or objectionable material to water.

Ponding, Filter.—See Pooling, Filter.

Pooling, Filter.—The formation of pools of sewage on the surface of filters caused by clogging.

Population Equivalent.—(1) The calculated population which would normally contribute the same amount of biochemical oxygen demand (BOD) per day. A common base is 0.167 lb. of 5-day BOD per capita per day. (2) For an industrial waste, the estimated number of people contributing sewage equal in strength to a unit volume of the waste or to some other unit involved in producing or manufacturing a particular commodity.

Pre-Aeration.—A preparatory treatment of sewage comprising aeration to remove gases, add oxygen, or promote flotation of grease, and aid coagulation.

Precipitation, Chemical.—Precipitation induced by addition of chemicals.

Pressure.—Pounds per square inch or square foot.

    Atmospheric.—The pressure exerted by the atmosphere at any point. Such pressure decreases the elevation of the point above sea level increases. One atmosphere is equal to 14.7 lb. per sq. in., 29.92 in. or 760 mm of mercury column or 33.90 ft. of water column at average sea level under standard conditions.

    Hydrostatic.—The pressure, expressed as a total force per unit of area, exerted by a body of water at rest.

    Negative.—A pressure less than the local atmospheric pressure at a given point.

Process.—A sequence of operations.

    Activated Sludge.—A biological sewage treatment process in which a mixture of sewage and activated sludge is agitated and aerated. The activated sludge is subsequently separated from the treated sewage (mixed liquor) by sedimentation, and wasted or returned to the process as needed. The treated sewage overflows the weir of the settling tank in which separation from the sludge takes place.

    Biological.—The process by which the life activities of bacteria, and other microorganisms in the search for food, break down complex organic materials into simple, more stable substances. Self-purification of sewage-polluted streams, sludge digestion, and all so-called secondary sewage treatments result from this process. Also called Biochemical Process.

Pump.—A device used to increase the head on a liquid.

    Booster.—A pump installed on a pipe line to raise the pressure of the water on the discharge side of the pump.

Centrifugal, Fluid.—A pump consisting of an impeller fixed on a rotating shaft and enclosed in a casing, having an inlet and a discharge connection. The rotating impeller creates pressure in the liquid by the velocity derived from centrifugal force.

Centrifugal, Screw.—A centrifugal pump having a screw-type impeller; may be axial-flow, or combined axial and radial-flow, type.

Centrifugal, Closed.—A centrifugal pump where the impeller is built with the vanes enclosed within circular disks.

Diaphragm.—A pump in which a flexible diaphragm, generally of rubber, is the operating part; it is fastened at the outer rim; when the diaphragm is moved in one direction, suction is exerted and when it is moved in the opposite direction, the liquid is forced through a discharge valve.

Double-Suction.—A centrifugal pump with suction pipes connected to the casing from both sides.

Duplex.—A reciprocating pump consisting of two cylinders placed side by side and connected to the same suction and discharge pipe, the pistons moving so that one exerts suction while the other exerts pressure, with the result that the discharge from the pump is continuous.

Horizontal Screw.—A pump with a horizontal cylindrical casing, in which operates a runner with radial blades, like those of a ship's propeller. The pump has a high efficiency at low heads and high discharges, and is used extensively in drainage work.

Mixed Flow.—A centrifugal pump in which the head is developed partly by centrifugal force and partly by the lift of the vanes on the liquid.

Open Centrifugal.—A centrifugal pump where the impeller is built with a set of independent vanes.

Propeller.—A centrifugal pump which develops most of its head by the propelling or lifting action of the vanes on the liquids.

Purification.—The removal, by natural or artificial methods, or objectionable matter from water.

Putrefaction.—Biological decomposition of organic matter with the production of ill-smelling products associated with anaerobic conditions.

Putrescibility. — (1) The relative tendency of organic matter to undergo decomposition in the absence of oxygen. (2) The susceptibility of waste waters, sewage, effluent, or sludge to putrefaction. (3) Term used in water or sewage analysis to define stability of a polluted water or raw or partially treated sewage.

Q

Quicklime.—A calcined material, the major part of which is calcium oxide or calcium oxide in natural association with a lesser amount of magnesium oxide, capable of slaking with water.

R

Rack.—An arrangement of parallel bars.

Bar.—A screen composed of parallel bars, either vertical or inclined, placed in a waterway to catch floating debris, and from which the screenings may be raked. Also called rack.

Coarse.—A rack with 3/4 inch to 6 inch spaces between bars.

Fine.—Generally used for a screen or rack which has openings of 3/32 to 3/16 inches. Some screens have less than 3/32 inch openings.

Radius, Hydraulic.—The cross-sectional area of a stream of water divided by the length of that part of its periphery in contact with its containing conduit; the ratio of area to wetted perimeter.

Rate.—The result of dividing one concrete number by another.

Filtration.—The rate of application of water or sewage to a filter, usually expressed in million gallons per acre per day, or gallons per minute per square foot.

Infiltration.—The rate, usually expressed in cubic feet per second, or million gallons per day per mile of waterway, at which ground water enters an infiltration ditch or gallery, drain, sewer, or other underground conduit.

Surface Settling.—Gallons per day per square foot of free horizontal water surface. Used in design of sedimentation tanks.

Reaeration.—The absorption of oxygen by a liquid, the dissolved oxygen content of which has been depleted.

Reaeration, Sludge.—The continuous aeration of sludge after its initial aeration in the activated sludge process.

Recirculation. — (1) The refiltration of all or a portion of the effluent in a high-rate trickling filter for the purpose of maintaining a uniform high rate through the filter. (2) The return of effluent to the incoming flow to reduce its strength.

Reduction.—The decrease in a specific variable.

Over-All.—The percentage reduction in the final effluent as compared to the raw sewage.

Percentage.—The ratio of material removed from water or sewage by treatment, to the material originally present (expressed as a percentage).

Sludge.—The reduction in the quantity and change in character of sewage sludge as the result of digestion.

Regulator.—A device or apparatus for controlling the quantity of sewage admitted to an intercepting sewer or a unit of a sewage treatment plant.

Reoxygenation.—The replenishment of oxygen in a stream from (1) dilution water entering stream, (2) biological reoxygenation through the activities of certain oxygen-producing plants, and (3) atmospheric reaction.

Residual, Chlorine.—See Chlorine, residual.

Rotor.—The member of an electric generator or water wheel which rotates.

S

Screen.—A device with openings, generally of uniform size, used to retain or remove suspended or floating solids in flowing water or sewage, and to prevent them from entering an intake or passing a given point in a conduit. The screening element may consist of parallel bars, rods, wires, grating, wire mesh, or perforated plate, and the openings may be of any shape, although they are generally circular or rectangular. The device may also be used to segregate granular material, such as sand, crushed rock, and soil, into various sizes.

Scum.—A mass of sewage matter which floats on the surface of sewage.

Second-Foot.—An abbreviated expression for cubic foot per second.

Sedimentation.—The process of subsidence and deposition of suspended matter carried by water, sewage, or other liquids, by gravity. It is usually accomplished by reducing the velocity of the liquid below the point where it can transport the suspended material. Also called Settling. See Precipitation, Chemical.

Final.—Settling of partly settled, flocculated or oxidized sewage in a final tank.

Plain.—The sedimentation of suspended matter in a liquid unaided by chemicals or other special means, and without provision for the decomposition of deposited solids in contact with the sewage.

Seeding, Sludge.—The inoculation of undigested sewage solids with sludge that has undergone decomposition, for the purpose of introducing favorable organisms, thereby accelerating the initial stages of digestion.

Self-Purification.—The natural processes of purification in a moving or still body of water whereby the bacterial content is reduced, the BOD is largely satisfied, the organic content is stabilized, and the dissolved oxygen returned to normal.

Sewage.—Largely the water supply of a community after it has been fouled by various uses. From the standpoint of source it may be a combination of the liquid or water-carried wastes from residences, business buildings, and institutions, together with those from industrial establishments, and with such ground water, surface water, and storm water as may be present.

    Domestic.—Sewage derived principally from dwellings, business buildings, institutions, and the like. (It may or may not contain ground water, surface water, or storm water.)

    Fresh.—Sewage of recent origin containing dissolved oxygen at the point of examination.

    Industrial.—Sewage in which industrial wastes predominate.

    Stable.—Sewage in which the organic matter has been stabilized.

    Raw.—Sewage prior to receiving any treatment.

    Sanitary.—(1) Domestic sewage with storm and surface water excluded. (2) Sewage discharging from the sanitary conveniences of dwellings (including apartment houses and hotels), office buildings, factories, or institutions. (3) The water supply of a community after it has been used and discharged into a sewer.

    Septic.—Sewage undergoing putrefaction under anaerobic conditions.

    Settled.—Sewage from which most of the settleable solids have been removed by sedimentation.

    Stale.—A sewage containing little or no oxygen, but as yet free from putrefaction.

Sewer.—A pipe or conduit. generally closed, but normally not flowing full, for carrying sewage and other waste liquids.

    Branch.—A sewer which receives sewage from a relatively small area, and discharges into a main sewer.

    Combined.—A sewer receiving both surface runoff and sewage.

    House.—A pipe conveying sewage from a single building to a common sewer or point of immediate disposal.

    Intercepting.—A sewer which receives dry-weather flow from a number of transverse sewers or outlets and frequently additional predetermined quantities of storm water (if from a combined system), and conducts such waters to a point for treatment or disposal.

    Lateral.—A sewer which discharges into a branch or other sewer and has no other common sewer tributary to it.

    Main. — (1) A sewer to which one or more branch sewers are tributary. Also called Trunk Sewer. (2) In plumbing, the public sewer in a street, alley, or other premises under the jurisdiction of a municipality.

    Sanitary.—A sewer which carries sewage and to which storm, surface, and ground waters are not intentionally admitted.

    Separate.—See Sewer, Sanitary.

    Storm.—A sewer which carries storm water and surface water, street wash and other wash waters, or drainage, but excludes sewage and industrial wastes. Also called Storm Drain.

    Trunk—A sewer which receives many tributary branches and serves a large territory. See Sewer, Main.

    Outfall.—A sewer which receives the sewage from a collecting system and carries it to a point of final discharge.

Outlet.—The point of final discharge of sewage or treatment plant effluent.

Sewerage.—A comprehensive term which includes facilities for collecting, pumping, treating, and disposing of sewage; the sewerage system and the sewage treatment works.

Shredder.—A device for size reduction.

    Screenings.—A device which disintegrates screenings.

    Sludge.—An apparatus to break down lumps in air-dried digested sludge.

Siphon.—A closed conduit, a portion of which lies above the hydraulic grade line. This results in a pressure less than atmospheric in that portion, and hence requires that a vacuum be created to start flow.

Skimmer, Grease.—A device for removing floating grease or scum from the surface of sewage in a tank.

Skimming.—The process of removing floating grease or scum from the surface of sewage in a tank.

Sleek.—The thin oily film usually present which gives characteristic appearance to the surface of water into which sewage or oily waste has discharged. Also termed slick.

Sloughing.—The phenomenon associated with trickling filters and contact aerators. whereby slime and solids accumulated in the media are discharged with the effluent.

Sludge.—The accumulated settled solids deposited from sewage or industrial wastes, raw or treated. in tanks or basins, and containing more or less water to form a semiliquid mass.

    Activated.—Sludge floc produced in raw or settled sewage by the growth of zoogleal bacteria and other organisms in the presence of dissolved oxygen, and accumulated in sufficient concentration by returning floc previously formed.

    Bulking.—A phenomenon that occurs in activated sludge plants whereby the sludge occupies excessive volumes and will not concentrate readily.

    Conditioning.—Treatment of liquid sludge preliminary to dewatering and drainability, usually by the addition of chemicals.

    Dewatering.—The process of removing a part of the water in sludge by any method, such as draining, evaporation, pressing, centrifuging, exhausting, passing between rollers, or acid flotation, with or without heat. It involves reducing from a liquid to a spadable condition rather than merely changing the density of the liquid (concentration) on the one hand or drying (as in a kiln) on the other.

    Digestion.—The process by which organic or volatile matter in sludge is gasified, liquefied, mineralized. or converted into more stable organic matter, through the activities of living organisms.

    Humus.—See **Humus**.

Solids.—Material in the solid state.

    Dissolved.—Solids which are present in solution.

    Nonsettleable.—Finely divided suspended solids which will not subside in quiescent water, sewage, or other liquid in a reasonable period. Such period is commonly, though arbitrarily, taken as two hours.

    Settleable.—Suspended solids which will subside in quiescent water, sewage, or other liquid in a reasonable period. Such period is commonly, though arbitrarily, taken as one hour. Also called Settling Solids.

    Suspended.—The quantity of material deposited when a quantity of water, sewage, or other liquid is filtered through an asbestos mat in a Gooch crucible.

    Total.—The solids in water, sewage, or other liquids; it includes the suspended solids (largely removable by filter paper) and the filterable solids (those which pass through filter paper).

Volatile.—The quantity of solids in water, sewage, or other liquid, lost on ignition of the total solids.

Squeegee.—(1) A device, generally with a soft rubber edge, used for dislodging and removing deposited sewage solids from the walls and bottoms of sedimentation tanks. (2) The metal blades attached to the lower arms of a clarifier mechanism to move the sludge along the tank bottom.

Stability.—The ability of any substance, such as sewage, effluent, or digested sludge, to resist putrefaction. It is the antonym of putrescibility.

Standard Methods.—Methods of analysis of water, sewage, and sludge approved by a Joint Committee of the American Public Health Association. American Water Works Association, and Federation of Sewage Works Associations.

Stator.—The stationary member of an electric generator or motor.

Sterilization.—The destruction of all living organisms, ordinarily through the agency of heat or of some chemical.

T

Tank.—A circular or rectangular vessel.

    Detritus.—A detention chamber larger than a grit chamber, usually with provision for removing the sediment without interrupting the flow of sewage. A settling tank of short detention period designed, primarily, to remove heavy settleable solids.

    Final Settling.—A tank through which the effluent from a trickling filter, or aeration or contact aeration tank flows for the purpose of removing the settleable solids.

    Flocculating.—A tank used for the formation of floc by the agitation of liquids.

    Imhoff.—A deep two-storied sewage tank originally patented by Karl Imhoff. consisting of an upper or continuous flow sedimentation chamber and a lower or sludge-digestion chamber. The floor of the upper chamber slopes steeply to trapped slots, through which solids may slide into the lower chamber. The lower chamber receives no fresh sewage directly, but is provided with gas vents and with means for drawing digested sludge from near the bottom.

    Primary Settling.—The first settling tank through which sewage is passed in a treatment works.

    Secondary.—A tank following a trickling filter or activated sludge aeration chamber.

    Sedimentation.—A tank or basin. in which water, sewage, or other liquid containing settleable solids, is retained for a sufficient time, and in which the velocity of flow is sufficiently low, to remove by gravity a part of the suspended matter. Usually, in sewage treatment, the detention period is short enough to avoid anaerobic decomposition. Also termed Settling or Subsidence Tank.

    Septic.—A single-story settling tank in which the settled sludge is in immediate contact with the sewage flowing through the tank, while the organic solids are decomposed by anaerobic bacterial action.

    Sludge-Digestion--See Digester.

Thickener, Sludge.—A type of sedimentation tank in which the sludge is permitted to settle, usually equipped with scrapers traveling along the bottom of the tank which push the settled sludge to a sump, from which it is removed by gravity or by pumping.

Treatment.—Any definite process for modifying the state of matter.

    Preliminary.—The conditioning of an industrial waste at its source prior 'to discharge, to remove or to neutralize substances injurious to sewers and treatment processes or to effect a partial reduction in load on the treatment process. In the treatment process, unit operations which prepare the liquor for subsequent major operations.

Primary.—The first major (sometimes the only) treatment in a sewage treatment works, usually sedimentation. The removal of a high percentage of suspended matter but little or no colloidal and dissolved matter.

Secondary.—The treatment of sewage by biological methods after primary treatment by sedimentation.

Sewage.—Any artificial process to which sewage is subjected in order to remove or alter its objectional constituents and thus to render it less offensive or dangerous.

Trap, Flame.—A device containing a fine metal gauze placed in a gas pipe, which prevents a flame from traveling back in the pipe and causing an explosion. See Arrester, Flame.

V

Venturi Meter.—A meter for measuring flow of water or other fluid through closed conduits or pipes, consisting of a Venturi tube and one of several proprietary forms of flow registering devices. The device was developed as a measuring device and patented by Clemens Herschel.

W

Waste Stabilization Pond.—Any pond, natural or artificial, receiving raw or partially treated sewage or waste, in which stabilization occurs due to sunlight, air, and microorganisms.

Water, Potable.—Water which does not contain objectionable pollution, contamination, minerals, or infection, and is considered satisfactory for domestic consumption.

Weir.—A dam with an edge or notch, sometimes arranged for measuring liquid flow.

    Effluent—A weir at the outflow end of a sedimentation basin or other hydraulic structure.

    Influent—A weir at the inflow end of a sedimentation basin.

    Rectangular.—A weir whose notch is rectangular in shape.

    Triangular.—A weir whose notch is triangular in shape, usually used to measure very small flows. Also called a V-notch.

    Peripheral.—The outlet weir in a circular settling tank, extending around the inside of its circumference and over which the effluent discharges.

    Rate.—See Loading, Weir.

Z

Zooglea.—A jelly-like matrix developed by bacteria, associated with growths in oxidizing beds.

www.ingramcontent.com/pod-product-compliance
Lightning Source LLC
Chambersburg PA
CBHW082149300426
44117CB00016B/2669